# INCARNATE

## THE BODY OF CHRIST IN AN AGE OF DISENGAGEMENT

## MICHAEL FROST

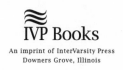

IVP Books

An imprint of InterVarsity Press
Downers Grove, Illinois

*InterVarsity Press*
*P.O. Box 1400, Downers Grove, IL 60515-1426*
*World Wide Web: www.ivpress.com*
*Email: email@ivpress.com*

*InterVarsity Press® is the book-publishing division of InterVarsity Christian Fellowship/USA®, a movement of students and faculty active on campus at hundreds of universities, colleges and schools of nursing in the United States of America, and a member movement of the International Fellowship of Evangelical Students. For information about local and regional activities, write Public Relations Dept., InterVarsity Christian Fellowship/USA, 6400 Schroeder Rd., P.O. Box 7895, Madison, WI 53707-7895, or visit the IVCF website at www.intervarsity.org.*

*All Scripture quotations, unless otherwise indicated, are taken from THE HOLY BIBLE, NEW INTERNATIONAL VERSION®, NIV® Copyright © 1973, 1978, 1984, 2011 by Biblica, Inc.™ Used by permission. All rights reserved worldwide.*

*While all stories in this book are true, some names and identifying information in this book have been changed to protect the privacy of the individuals involved.*

*Cover design: Cindy Kiple*
*Interior design: Beth Hagenberg*
*Image: Face in the Crowd by Evelyn Williams. Private Collection/The Bridgeman Art Library.*

*ISBN 978-0-8308-4417-3 (print)*
*ISBN 978-0-8308-8405-6 (digital)*

*Printed in the United States of America* ∞

**Library of Congress Cataloging-in-Publication Data**
Frost, Michael, 1961-
  Incarnate : the body of Christ in an age of disengagement / Michael
Frost.
    pages cm
  Includes bibliographical references.
  ISBN 978-0-8308-4417-3 (pbk. : alk. paper)
  1. Incarnation. 2. Christian life. 3. Mission of the church. 4.
Missions—Theory. I. Title.
  BV4509.5.F755 2014
  261—dc23
                                                                    2013046585

| P | 18 | 17 | 16 | 15 | 14 | 13 | 12 | 11 | 10 | 9 | 8 | 7 | 6 | 5 | 4 | 3 | 2 | 1 |
|---|----|----|----|----|----|----|----|----|----|---|---|---|---|---|---|---|---|---|
| Y | 29 | 28 | 27 | 26 | 25 | 24 | 23 | 22 | 21 | 20 | 19 | 18 | 17 | 16 | 15 | 14 | | | |

*For my wife, Carolyn,*
*whose practice of genuine presence*
*and embodied*
*love knows no bounds*

# Contents

# Introduction

## Defleshing the Human Experience

*In the near future we'll only be able to communicate
through devices. Actual human contact will be
outlawed by the Apple iCourt.*

JIM CARREY

᚛

I t might seem odd to start a book about incarnation with a description of its opposite—excarnation—but bear with me. In order to understand the urgent need for incarnational living, an awareness of the excarnated nature of contemporary life is necessary. Technically, excarnation, also known as *defleshing*, refers to the ancient practice of removing the flesh and organs of the dead, leaving only the bones. In some cultures excarnation is conducted by natural means, which involves leaving a body exposed for animals to scavenge. In others it is purposefully undertaken by defleshing the corpse by hand, which can leave scraping marks on the bones, a telltale sign for archaeologists.

Excarnation was common practice in the late British Neolithic period, and usually performed by natural means. On Orkney,

Scotland, the Isbister Tomb contains the skeletons of 340 people. The skeletons were disarticulated and incomplete, the bones bleached and weathered, making it very probable that the bodies had been laid out once on mortuary platforms, exposed to the elements and birds of prey, before ultimate interment. Isbister is also known as the "Tomb of the Eagles," because they found the talons and bones of sea eagles with the human bones. Anthropologists have surmised that the sea eagle would have been a totem for these people, as it represents flight and travel, symbols which are boldly associated with the journey to an afterlife.

On the other hand, defleshing manually was not uncommon in medieval Europe, where the flesh from the bodies of deceased monarchs and military commanders was removed so that the bones could be transported hygienically from distant lands back home. Originally a Germanic practice, it was called *mos Teutonicus* (literally in English "the German custom") and led to the veneration of various bits and pieces of kings and saints right across Christendom.

Further afield, precontact Hawaiians ritually defleshed the bones of high-ranking nobles (*ali'i*) so that they could be interred in reliquaries for later veneration. The famous British explorer Captain Cook, who the Hawaiians had first believed to be the god Lono, met this fate after he was killed in Hawaii in a fight with the locals during his third exploratory voyage in the Pacific in 1779.

I mention all this not merely to highlight an archaic custom but to suggest that while the defleshing of corpses is no longer in vogue, we currently find ourselves in a time in history where another kind of excarnation occurs, an existential kind in which we are being convinced to embrace an increasing disembodied presence in our world. This kind of excarnation is based on a body-spirit dualism wherein less value and influence is placed on the physical and enormous importance is accrued to the spiritual. What we do with our bodies is of lesser interest to us than what we do with our spirits, an increasingly pervasive stance in Western society and one that is exacerbated by a Platonic form of Christianity.

Historically, excarnation was a means by which the dead were honored: the dust-to-dust association of leaving the body to be defleshed by animals, the hygienic transportation of military dead for proper mourning, the ritual defleshing of Hawaiian nobles. These were carefully chosen acts, sacramental occasions, that made meaning for death and reflected the cultural values of the living. Compare that with the kind of excarnation we're observing today: the neglect of our embodiedness, the denial of aging and death, the strategic defleshing of our opponents on virtual fields of battle. What was intended to honor the dead has become the unconscious habit of the living. Practicing excarnation on the dead gives meaning to life; practicing excarnation among the living is destructive, violent, death-bringing.

In his incendiary 1906 novel *The Jungle*, about life in the meat-packing plants of the Chicago stockyard, Upton Sinclair revealed that meat packers had developed the first industrial assembly line long before Henry Ford adapted it to automobile production. It could have been more accurately termed a *disassembly line*, requiring nearly eighty separate jobs, from killing an animal to processing its meat for sale. "Killing gangs" held jobs like "knockers," "rippers," "leg breakers" and "gutters." The animal carcasses moved continuously on hooks until processed into fresh, smoked, salted, pickled and canned meats. The organs, bones, fat and other scraps ended up as lard, soap and fertilizer. Sinclair quipped that the workers said that the meat-packing companies "used everything but the squeal."[1]

In this book we will look at the ways contemporary society has defleshed the human experience, disembodying others by treating people as objects or ideas. Like the disassembly line described by Sinclair, contemporary life is drawing us further and further along the process of excarnation, as evidenced by cruel and ruthless ideological debates on television, as well as the use of blogs, Facebook, Twitter and other social media, to attack our opponents, and worse. We will explore the disembodiment of morality, including the effects of pornography, online gaming, zombie and vampire movies, and more. We will examine the disconnect many feel from their sense of place, which has led to the spiritual homelessness described by Peter Berger, where modern people belong everywhere but nowhere.

From a Christian perspective we also will look at how the trend toward excarnation has influenced the church and led to a disembodying of our faith, the transfer of our religious life out of bodily forms of ritual, worship and practice, so that it comes more and more to reside "in the head" and results in the loss of liturgy and sacred time. Behind this, of course, lies the excarnation of our theology, the exaltation of disengaged reason as the road to knowledge, the emergence of disenchantment as the mother of "causal laws," leading to us perceiving the world as mechanistic, which in turn raises questions about how we're to read Scripture. Ultimately, all this has resulted in a disembodied approach to the mission of the church, a drift toward nonincarnational expressions, where disembodied advocacy is preferable to the dirt and worms and compost of localized service. We see this in the preference for short-term mission trips and "treasure hunting" approaches to evangelism, where we are expected to minister to strangers we'll never see again.

I believe that in a time of disengagement and excarnation, the body of Christ is required all the more to embrace a more thoroughly embodied faith, a truly placed way of living that mirrors the incarnational lifestyle of Jesus. Now, more than ever, it seems, such a call to incarnational living needs to be heeded.

In his wrenching vision of American moral life, *Lost Memory of Skin*, novelist Russell Banks takes to task the plugged-in, tuned-out

Internet culture lost in the misty zone between reality and imagery, no longer able to tell the difference, and explores the terrible, dehumanizing consequences of choosing to live this way. Banks's story is about the Kid, a sex offender and online porn addict, living in a makeshift camp on the uninhabitable outskirts of an airport, under a causeway, far from civil society. All the other residents are also sex offenders. The Kid's only real friend is his pet iguana, Iggy. He is estranged from his mother, who subjected him to a parade of disinterested boyfriends and then abandoned him once he was convicted of his crime. Throughout the course of the story we come to see how dreadfully damaging the Kid's addiction to pornography has been. The title, *Lost Memory of Skin*, refers to the way real flesh has been supplanted by the virtual kind. The Kid is still a virgin and knows more about the touch of iguana skin, and the lousy acting of porn stars, than he does about anything actually human.

There is a disconnect between the imagination and the flesh, a disconnect that is serving to produce the most perilous and creepy repercussions for contemporary society. We bring the most human impulses to the least human means of expressing them, and we may not see the damage we do until it becomes irrevocable. This disconnect is just one of many of the central human experiences—sexuality, politics, religion and more—that are taking place not in our bodies but entirely in our heads. We are, in a word, becoming dangerously excarnate.

Ultimately, it's my grave concern that the excarnate nature of the Christian faith in the West today means we are creating new generations of believers who know more than they choose, who understand things they never act upon, who discern ideas they never use. Like the Kid, they are like virgins who have seen everything but only know the touch of an iguana's skin.

# 1

# Rootless, Disengaged and Screen Addicted

*I have no connections here;*
*only gusty collisions, rootless seedlings*
*forced into bloom, that collapse.*

MARGE PIERCY

🔲

The core idea of the Christian faith is the incarnation: God took on flesh and dwelled among us. To other religions such an idea is considered odd or, worse, inconceivable or, even worse, blasphemous. And yet as centrally as we hold the idea of the incarnation, there is a grave danger that we are leaving the implications of great idea behind us. Whereas Jesus Christ was God incarnate and his church was called to an incarnational lifestyle, today we find ourselves drifting toward excarnation—the defleshing of our faith. We have been moving through a disembodying process that has left us feeling rootless and disengaged, connected to our world more and more through screens rather than face to face.

Cultural commentator Richard Sennett has claimed that the primary architectural emblem of contemporary life is the airport departure lounge.[1] It's a telling symbol and reveals something of the

excarnate nature of things. The departure lounge is full of people
who don't belong where they currently find themselves and whose
interactions with others are fleeting, perfunctory and trivial. Airport
lounges are highly depersonalized spaces. Even those of us who
travel a lot have difficulty telling one airport lounge from another.
They are bland, liminal places, and their lack of specificity makes
us yearn for somewhere real, for our destination. Nobody *belongs*
in an airport lounge. Most people make the experience bearable by
focusing on their mobile devices, thanks to the recent innovation
of airports providing free Wi-Fi access (even airports don't want
you to belong in their lounges). Travelers' heads are elsewhere,
checking email or social media, listening to music or watching
films or television programs on tablets or phones.

There is also a very obvious, yet unspoken, etiquette in airport
lounges. There's no yelling and screaming, even when passengers
become frustrated with airline service. No one even talks loudly.
There is a quiet order to the environment. But none of this behavior
is enforced by signs that say "Don't talk too loudly," "Don't move
the chairs," "Don't occupy more than one seat." These things
happen due to an invisible hand of design. The environment has
been manipulated to elicit certain behavior. The seats are arranged
so that people talk to those who are close, and they don't shout
across the room. This makes the departure lounge a nonworld of
individual choice and endless mobility, and we reach it by under-
taking an arduous assembly-line process of check-ins, security
screenings, moving walkways and internal skyrail trips.

In a sense the airport departure lounge is the end point in our
disassembly line, as we move endlessly, lining up in zigzagged
queues, each stage stripping back our sense of belonging, our sense
of rootedness in place and culture. This is even symbolized in the
removal of various items of clothing, wristwatches and laptops
during security screening. By the time we reach our gate lounge we

have become less truly present in our own space. But of course, I speak of this not merely as a problem for air travelers. Richard Sennett sees the gate lounge as a symbol for all contemporary life. So too does the Polish sociologist Zygmunt Bauman, who considers *tourism* as a primary metaphor for modern living.[2] Like tourists, the lives of liberated Westerners are marked by mobility and impermanence, a looseness of ties to place and people. This, Bauman contends, gives way to "grazing behavior," an endless sampling of experience that shies away from strict commitment to any one style, ideology or belief.[3]

In an excarnate world there is a discernible lack of commitment or loyalty to any one worldview. Ever seen tourists returning from a vacation in India sporting red bindis between their eyebrows, and wearing beer-stained T-shirts from Planet Hollywood Mumbai? Why do you think airports are crammed with faux-regional restaurants like Bubba Gump's Shrimp Co. or On the Border Cantina? We know we're not on the bayou or in Tijuana, but, like tourists, we're willing to sample a little hyper-real cuisine while we belong nowhere and have no sense of attachment to our surroundings. In fact, the next time you're sitting on a fake Brentwood chair in an airport TGI Friday's under a red-and-white candy-striped awning, surrounded by brass rails and fake stained glass, your meal lit by faux Tiffany lamps, your server wearing a red-and-white striped soccer shirt, remind yourself you're not actually *anywhere* right now. Your body might be in the airport lounge, but your mind is somewhere else—on social media, playing online games, watching Fox News on the airport screens, dreaming of somewhere else. You've realized your primary status in contemporary society as a disembodied one, free to roam, free to stray, free to be, well, free.

All this is captured brilliantly and with wit and humanity in the film *Up in the Air* (2009). Directed by Jason Reitman and cowritten by Reitman and Sheldon Turner, based on the 2001 novel of the

same name by Walter Kirn, *Up in the Air* is about a corporate down-
sizer Ryan Bingham (George Clooney) and his business travels
across America. Set mainly in airports and offices in St Louis, De-
troit, Omaha, Las Vegas and Miami, the film follows Bingham's isolated life and the warped philosophies he has developed to justify
himself. Reitman captures America's current anxieties and touches
on larger themes of mass unemployment, cultural alienation and
technology as a crutch. But ultimately, it's really an expertly done
character study that's as eloquent about today's executive culture as
Billy Wilder's *The Apartment* was in 1960. It is a brutal, desolate film,
and a superb existential lesson in contemporary socioeconomics. It
might well have been written and directed by Zygmunt Bauman, so
perfectly does it illustrate his thesis regarding the grazing mentality
of contemporary culture.

Ryan Bingham keeps himself "on the road," in the old parlance;
literally "up in the air," as he constantly travels from one corporate
meeting to the next (where he routinely fires staff from downsizing
companies). He justifies it this way:

> The slower we move the faster we die. Make no mistake,
> moving is living. Some animals were meant to carry each
> other, to live symbiotically over a lifetime. Star crossed lovers,
> monogamous swans. We are not swans. We are sharks.[4]

While training a new assistant, Natalie Keener (Anna Kendrick),
on the most expedient way through airport security, he counsels
her, "Never get behind old people. Their bodies are littered with
hidden metal and they never seem to appreciate how little time they
have left. Bingo, Asians. They pack light, travel efficiently, and they
have a thing for slipon shoes. Gotta love 'em."

When Natalie tells him he's being racist, he replies, "I'm like my
mother, I stereotype. It's faster." The irony of claiming his relationship with his mother as the basis for treating people as objects

is sharp. What really matters to Bingham is speed. At one point he tells Natalie that checking luggage is a pointless time waster: "You know how much time you lose by checking in? Thirty five minutes a flight. I travel 270 days a year. That's 157 hours. That makes seven days. You're willing to throw away an entire week on that?"

As we discover, Bingham has very little on which to spend that time he saves in airports. He has no family, no friends, no commitments. He launches into a convenient sexual relationship with an equally driven executive, with no emotional strings attached. Ryan Bingham is totally excarnated, a disembodied soul who navigates his way through airports and sleeps in impersonal hotel rooms while championing the virtues of temporariness and mobility. He is grazing on experience, committing to none. In one telling conversation with Natalie he reveals that his life's goal is to earn ten million miles on his airline's mileage program. He's not saving his miles for a vacation in Hawaii or the south of France. He just wants to crack the elusive ten million: "I'd be the seventh person to do it. More people have walked on the moon. You get lifetime executive status. You get to meet the chief pilot, Maynard Finch. And they put your name on the side of a plane."

We know this sounds pathetic, but I suspect that our great fear as we listen to Ryan Bingham is that he might represent all of us in some way. Sure, he's an extreme version, but those of us who find our lives shaped by freeways and airports, hotel rooms and dormitory suburbs, who have no time, who never belong (truly belong) anywhere or to anyone, have been through the disassembly line too. Our culture's obsession with so-called freedom and mobility has stripped our flesh away and we can no longer feel the elements or touch our surroundings. This was epitomized by celebrity tweeter Nicole Richie recently when she commented that her husband, Good Charlotte front man Joel Madden, would pay more attention to her if she dressed up as a smart phone. People like Madden are

present but not available to those around them. They pay more attention to their phones. I recently attended a concert where one of
the backing singers was filming the whole performance, including
himself, on his phone and Facebooking the experience to the band's
fans. Present but not available. Excarnate!

## DISENGAGEMENT AND OBJECTIFICATION

The second expression of the excarnate experience of contemporary
life is our disengagement from society and our capacity for the
objectification of others. As long ago as the seventeenth century,
modernism gave people the intellectual capacity to control their
world by disengaging from it, via the process of objectification. To
objectify something is to deprive it of its normative force for us, or
at least to bracket the force it has for us in our lives. In other words,
if we take an aspect of life that once had defined meanings or set
standards for us, and we now take a neutral stance toward it,
without meaning or normative force, we can speak of objectifying
it. Charles Taylor says,

> The ideal of disengagement defines a certain—typically
> modern—notion of freedom, as the ability to act on one's own,
> without interference or subordination to outside authority. . . .
> The great attraction of these ideals, all the more powerful in
> that this understanding of the agent is woven into a host of
> modern practices—economic, scientific, technological,
> psycho-therapeutic, and so on—lends great weight and cre-
> dence to the disengaged image of the self.[5]

Modernism gave us the ability to disengage from our world, objectify it and gain mastery over it. But, as postmodern philosophers
argued, this arrogant lust for disengagement and objectification has
also been our undoing. Now, the most commonly experienced form
of such disengagement is not our objectification of nature or science

as such, but that of other people. When we wish to control others we disengage from them and objectify them as concrete and separate objects. You see this in how commonly we turn people into things by talking about them in the third person or using stereotypes to describe them (He's one of *them*. She's just an unthinking *Arminian*. Well, you *Baptists* would think that!). We also use nominalization—the turning of verbs into nouns, by adding "ion." Thus, we say to friends and allies, "Let's act!" But to those from whom we've disengaged we say, "Action will be required." It's difficult not to feel objectified when someone tells you, "Consideration of this would be appreciated," rather than, "Would you please consider this?" More than that, note how often people turn ideas into symbols and metaphors, and then treat them like things. For example, Calvinism can be an objectified thing by those who don't subscribe to it, and you can hear them speak of it as a metaphoric object so they can then discuss it at arm's length more easily.

Objectifying creates distance, separating us from the person and their ideas. It allows us to discuss them and use extensions of the metaphoric world to scrutinize them objectively. It also allows us to distance ourselves from culpable actions or unfair caricatures. Such objectification depersonalizes them and almost always leads to discounting, downplaying, victimization and bullying. I could quote certain scholars' discussion of the emerging church here. Or various pastors' caricature of female church leaders. Or any number of theological or ecclesial debates and controversies. Or any number of Facebook threads for that matter. As we will see later, when leaders are anxious about the times they live in, they resort to them-and-us thinking.

In late 2012 the fast-food chain Chick-fil-A became the center of controversy following comments made by chief operating officer Dan Cathy opposing same-sex marriage. This followed reports that Chick-fil-A's charitable arm had contributed millions in donations to political organizations that oppose LGBT rights. In response LGBT rights activists called for protests and boycotts of the chain, while conservative Christians rallied in support by eating at the restaurants on an appointed "Chick-fil-A Appreciation Day." The media storm that surrounded this controversy ensured that eating a chicken sandwich (or not) had become a political act.

What was not known at the time but was revealed the following year was that in the heat of the dispute, Dan Cathy made a surprise call to Shane Windmeyer, a nationally recognized LGBT leader and the executive director of Campus Pride. Windmeyer disclosed what happened next in his article "Dan and Me: My Coming Out as a Friend of Dan Cathy and Chick-fil-A." Assuming Cathy had rung him to give him a piece of his mind, Windmeyer was cautious at first, but after an hour on the phone he began to relax. Cathy was calling because he genuinely wanted to understand the arguments behind the LGBT case. This call led to others and then a number of in-person meetings. Dan Cathy had never before had such dialogue with any member of the LGBT community. Windmeyer said it was awkward at times, but Cathy was always genuine and kind. Windmeyer wrote,

> It is not often that people with deeply held and completely opposing viewpoints actually risk sitting down and listening to one another. We see this failure to listen and learn in our government, in our communities and in our own families. Dan Cathy and I would, together, try to do better than each of us had experienced before.[6]

To his credit, never once did Dan or anyone from Chick-fil-A ask for Campus Pride to stop protesting Chick-fil-A. On the contrary, the phone calls and meetings were a sincere attempt at listening and understanding. Cathy confessed that he had been naive to the issues at hand and the unintended impact of his company's actions.

And he directed his staff to provide Windmeyer with access to internal documents related to the funding of anti-LGBT groups. Windmeyer continued,

> Through all this, Dan and I shared respectful, enduring communication and built trust. His demeanor has always been one of kindness and openness. Even when I continued to directly question his public actions and the funding decisions, Dan embraced the opportunity to have dialogue and hear my perspective. He and I were committed to a better understanding of one another. Our mutual hope was to find common ground if possible, and to build respect no matter what. We learned about each other as people with opposing views, not as opposing people.[7]

Ultimately, Dan Cathy and Chick-fil-A changed their policies for funding charitable organizations, but he also found a new friend, and in doing so showed us what the refusal to give in to stereotyping and objectification looks like. It is generous, warm, hospitable and gracious.

## SCREEN CULTURE AND VIRTUAL REALITY

To compound all this subordination of the body, the rise of the influence of the Internet has contributed radically to the increasingly excarnate experience of life today. This is the third broad expression of excarnate culture. We debate or mock those with whom we disagree on blogs and in social media without ever engaging them face to face. We refer to people who have connected with us on Facebook as our "friends" without necessarily having ever met them. In fact, nothing is more subversively excarnate than the pressure to objectify a stranger as a "friend."

Many teens recognize that they and their friends and family are increasingly tethered to their electronic gadgets, and a substantial number express a desire to disconnect sometimes. A recent study found that 41 percent of teens describe themselves as "addicted" to their phones.[8] Forty-three percent of teens wish that they could "unplug," and more than a third wish they could go back to a time when there was no Facebook. Some teens get frustrated by how attached their friends and parents are to their own devices. For example, 28 percent of those whose parents have a mobile device say they consider their parents addicted to their gadgets, and 21 percent of all teens say they wish their parents spent less time with their cell phones and other devices. Nearly half (45%) of teens say they sometimes get frustrated with their friends for texting, surfing the Internet or checking their social networking sites while they're hanging out together.

A more insidious example of the impact of screen time and virtual reality is the effect that sexual addiction fueled by online pornography has on its sufferers. In his provocative ebook *The Demise of Guys: Why Boys Are Struggling and What We Can Do About It*, psychologist Philip Zimbardo says that an addiction to video games and online porn have created a generation of shy, socially awkward, emotionally removed and risk-averse young men who are unable (and unwilling) to navigate the complexities and risks inherent to real-life relationships, school and employment. Zimbardo believes young men today are suffering from a new form of "arousal addiction" that has led to a general loss of motivation and put negative pressure on their capacity for meaningful social and romantic attachment:

> The most popular answers from our 20,000-person survey was that widespread hardcore Internet porn is wreaking havoc on relationships. Women said it's made guys emotionally unavailable, and guys said it made them less interested in pursuing a relationship in the first place.[9]

This is the excarnate world we live in. And for every fictional example, like Ryan Bingham, Philip Zimbardo can introduce us to a host of real-life examples. If excarnate culture has led to us living life "up in the air," struggling with the "lost memory of skin," then it has also given us televangelist scandals and tawdry tales of the behind-the-scenes world of TBN or the Crystal Cathedral. It has seeped into our everyday thinking in the church as well. We drive our SUVs across town to churches in neighborhoods we don't live in (and don't want to). We send SMSs and check Twitter during the sermon, and then we download our favorite celebrity preacher's sermon as a podcast to listen to during the week. We engage in online discussions by posting smug and condescending remarks about those unseen, unknown folks with whom we disagree. We sign petitions and change our Facebook profile picture to show our support for various causes without any thought of getting involved personally. We are outraged by those who manipulate child soldiers in Africa or who traffic sex workers from Central Europe, but we don't open our homes to our own neighbors, let alone those with no home at all. And this isn't to even mention the prevalence of online porn usage by churchgoing men, including male clergy.

These days even some church leaders themselves are intentionally excarnate, appearing only on screen via satellite links, beamed in from the mother church, multiplied and digitized for a consumer audience. It's as though the pastor now becomes the new icon in the Protestant worship service, and if that's true, it's hard to see how the video-based multisite church can't tend toward idolatry, pride and self-promotion—even where the ambition of spreading the gospel is genuine. In 1986 I remember watching a scene in Peter Weir's film *The Mosquito Coast* where a creepy missionary forces the native villagers to sit in church and watch him preaching via simulcast on television sets in the place of the pulpit. His screen-based omnipresence left the villagers in awe of him, but it rightly evoked contempt from movie audiences in the 1980s. I thought it was ludicrous. Little did we know (including Paul Theroux and

Paul Schrader, who wrote the novel and the screenplay respectively) that this would one day be a common practice in churches across America. Theroux and Schrader only imagined it working with gape-jawed Central American natives mesmerized by the new technology. How would they explain it working in Seattle or Los Angeles today?

## LIKE THE HONOLULU GARDENS

In his book *Living Holiness* John Thomson points out that the Christian faith in the United States has become totally abstracted and disembodied. He says that rather than embodying God's story of grace and the good life, the church "has been severely diminished due to a preoccupation with ideas and abstractions at the expense of such embodiment."[10] I'm inclined to agree, and yet, as Stanley Hauerwas says, "The story [of God] is not merely told but embodied in a people's habits that form and are formed in worship, governance, and morality."[11] Here's where I think the church can be the alternative and the antidote to the excarnational impulses in society today. Rather than mirroring these impulses and tendencies, the Christian community could reveal to the world around us what a truly earthed, communal, relational, embodied experience of life can be like.

On a stopover from Sydney to Los Angeles, I found myself biding time in transit in Honolulu International Airport. It is, to my amazement, set among a series of lush gardens, designed, as I later discovered, by Richard Tongg in 1962. Three cultural gardens display the influence of the Hawaiian, Chinese and Japanese heritages on the state of Hawaii and are connected by meandering pathways, bridges and stepping stones. Goldfish splash about in lakes amid lotus and lily pads in the Chinese garden. Pine and bamboo trees along with other native Chinese flowering trees are strategically placed among craggy rock formations. The Japanese section features a zigzag bridge (which keeps away evil) under which colorful carp create patterns in the ponds surrounded by sculptured pine and weeping willow trees. In the Hawaiian gardens, there are quiet lagoons filled with koi, gurgling springs and waterfalls cascading down lava walls. In the tropical setting, banana, coconut, hala (pandanus) and kukui (candlenut) trees shade ti plants, exotic ferns, such as the lauae and monstera, and eye-catching flowers, white ginger, red torch ginger and bird of paradise. At night, luau torches illuminate the garden where glass ball floats hang from the huge branches of the monkeypod trees.

All this is visible from the windows of the concourse, which is otherwise like any other airport in the world. As my fellow travelers played Angry Birds on their iPads or stared aimlessly into space, I was unable to take my eyes from the gorgeous verdant gardens outside. Real birds flittered about. The movement of fish sent ripples across the ponds. Willow branches swayed in the breeze. A gardener was clipping a pine tree. The grass was tropically green, the soil volcanic black. From my vantage point in the sterile environment of an airport concourse, Richard Tongg's gardens were like metaphoric oxygen to my soul. Even though I couldn't smell them or breathe them through the security-glazed and insulated airport windows, the gardens outside were the perfect antidote to the air-conditioned, culturally nonspecific interior of my departure lounge.

Those gardens made me yearn for dirt and worms and compost. They made me hunger for *place*. They reminded me that the grazing life of the tourist is no metaphor for real living, that bouncing across the top of faux Hawaiian culture (or any such culture for that matter) is meaningless. Those little gardens surrounded by a veritable sea of concrete runways and metallic hangars were islands that cried out to me that embodied truth and faithful habits, and liturgy and enacted morality, and face-to-face relationship were the real stuff.

Like the gardens at Honolulu International Airport, the church is to be just that—dirt and worms and compost compared to the sterility of the departure lounges of the excarnate life. We are to embody faith and life in the company of those who've fallen for rootlessness and grazing behavior, for disengagement and objectification, for screen culture and virtual reality. If we are to be like the Japanese gardens in the Honolulu airport, it will require a recommitment to embodied forms of witness bolstered by a profoundly incarnational theology. If we can do this we might just become salt and light in a bland and darkened world.

# 2

# The Schizophrenic Sense of Self

*In the last analysis, faith is not the sum of our beliefs
or a way of speaking or a way of thinking; it is a way of living
and can be articulated only in a living practice.*

BRENNAN MANNING

**N**aomi Shihab Nye is a Palestinian-American poet based in San Antonio. In her beautiful story "Gate A-4" (better known as "Wandering Around an Albuquerque Airport Terminal"), she describes her encounter with an older woman in full traditional Palestinian dress crumpled on the floor of a gate lounge in the Albuquerque airport, wailing loudly. The distressed woman's plane had been delayed, but given her limited English she thought the flight had been canceled entirely.

She needed to be in El Paso for some major medical treatment the following day and was afraid she would miss it. Nye explained in Arabic that everything would be okay. The plane would be late, but they would still get to El Paso. The story then describes the charming scene that played out in the otherwise sterile environment of the gate lounge. Naomi Shihab Nye allowed the older woman to use her cell phone to call the woman's son, who was meeting her in El Paso. Then, just for fun, they called her other sons. Then Nye called her Palestinian-born father, and he and the older woman had a conversation in Arabic and discovered they had ten friends in common. Then the woman pulled out a bag of homemade mamool cookies, which Nye describes as "little powdered-sugar crumbly mounds stuffed with dates and nuts," and began offering them to all the women at the gate. Everyone took one, and soon they were all covered in powdered sugar and smiling and laughing. Nye concludes,

> And I noticed my new best friend—by now we were holding hands—had a potted plant poking out of her bag, some medicinal thing, with green furry leaves. Such an old country tradition. Always carry a plant. Always stay rooted to somewhere.
>
> And I looked around that gate of late and weary ones and thought, This is the world I want to live in. The shared world. Not a single person in that gate—once the crying of confusion stopped—seemed apprehensive about any other person. They took the cookies. I wanted to hug all those other women, too.
>
> This can still happen anywhere. Not everything is lost.[1]

This can still happen. Even in the nowhereness of the Albuquerque airport, embodied community, generosity, laughter, culture, food and family can burst forth like green shoots through the cracks in the concrete. But it's rare. And that's the problem. The drift toward rootlessness and disengagement seems relentless, and the church, sadly, is finding itself drawn in the same direction.

You see this drift in your own life when you consider highly personalized, private times with God are of a supremely higher spiritual order than anything you could encounter in community in the physical world. Furthermore, when your understanding of Christian worship is that it takes place primarily in your imagination stimulated by the singing of intensely emotional songs, rather than in embodied liturgy and practice, you might be enjoying an excarnate faith.

You know you are living an excarnate form of religion when your adoration of the God you encounter in the place of rigorous theological study has superseded anything you could experience in the service of others or the place of real physical connection with the poor or the lost.

You know excarnation is taking a hold on you when your most stimulating interactions with others are the brief comments you make or receive on social media rather than the more challenging face-to-face conversations you have with friends over a meal.

You know you are living an increasingly excarnate life when knowledge that you once carried in deeply meaningful bodily forms lies more and more in the "head" or the "heart." Then you are literally defleshing your Christian experience, excarnating your spirituality of any corporeal or active expression. In all, I suggest Christianity has become an out-of-body experience—personalized, privatized, customized—and it is being dished up to us by a clergy increasingly disconnected from an incarnational expression of faith. And yet, as Canadian philosopher Charles Taylor pointedly remarks, this is contrary to the very nature of our faith: "Christianity, as the faith of the Incarnate God, is denying something essential to itself as long as it remains wedded to forms which excarnate."[2]

We need look no further than the Sunday services of many churches to find evidence of increasingly excarnate Christianity. I find myself astonished at times to observe the intensity with which some Christians sing the indecipherable lyrics of some contemporary worship songs. A currently popular church song, *The Stand*, includes the verse,

So I'll walk upon salvation
Your spirit alive in me
This life to declare your promise
My soul now to stand.

Whenever I'm in church when it's being sung, I always turn to the person next to me and ask him or her what "my soul now to stand" actually means. No one can tell me. They just close their eyes and keep singing.

I'm not intending to ridicule this song, but because I don't know what the words mean I find it difficult to sing it with much gusto. Interestingly, several enthusiastic worshipers have told me that they don't think much about the meaning of the lyrics, allowing themselves to be caught up in enthusiasm for the God it is directed toward. They are more moved by the cadence and rhythm of song and the feelings they evoke than any lyrical content. This is an extremely excarnate form of worship. When the worship of God happens only in our heads, with no bodily involvement, we are heading in a disconcerting direction. As British author, Nick Page says,

> I'm not knocking emotion. [It is] is part of our response to God. A non-emotional Christian is someone who has forgotten how to feel; but, equally, a completely emotional Christian is someone who has forgotten how to think. Too often worship times are judged, not on whether people were changed or challenged or renewed, but on the response of the crowd, the "buzz" in the building. This is not a reliable indicator of the presence of God. I frequently feel intense emotions when Watford scores a goal. But I wouldn't claim that God had much to do with it.[3]

Furthermore, Roger Helland and Leonard Hjalmarson make the case that the church's approach to teaching reflects its excarnate nature as well. They fear that evangelicalism as a movement, with its high value on biblical teaching, can be drawn to an excarnational, knowledge-based approach to spiritual formation, living in a world of ideas and words that primarily only reaches people's heads.[4] They quote Doug Pagitt, saying, "I believe the knowledge-based spiritual formation of the twentieth century has so reduced the call of Jesus to right belief that many become confused about why mere profession of belief does not bring change."[5]

When you consider that the average Sunday worship service in the evangelical world consists of standing still and *imagining* God as we sing, and sitting still and *thinking about* God as we hear biblical sermons, you can see how we are reinforcing a weekly rhythm of engagement with God *in our heads*!

## DUALISM IS FOUNDATIONAL TO EXCARNATION

The philosophical foundation of excarnation can be found in Christian dualism, a worldview that is so pervasive and so taken for granted that revealing its manifestations in the church and beyond are both too easy and too difficult. I first addressed this in a book I wrote many years ago, *Seeing God in the Ordinary*, and I revisited it in *The Shaping of Things to Come*, where I identified dualism as one of the primary problems of the evangelical church.[6]

Many years ago, when my daughters were young, we were traipsing through an overgrown cemetery not far from our home, reading the names of those buried and working out their age when they died according to the dates on their headstones. One of my daughters was struggling to come to terms with the idea of people's bodies being buried beneath our feet and kept querying this fact. When I asked what part of it she wasn't able to understand, she replied, "If their bodies are under the ground, where have their voices gone?"

I stammered out some inadequate response about their voices going to join with the voice of God in heaven, and that seemed to either satisfy her or so totally confuse her she preferred to skip off and pick wildflowers and think no further about it.

The idea that our voices can't be silenced by being buried in a box seems charming, even poetic, but what did I mean when I told her our voices go to join God's in heaven? Had my daughter intuited something about the human soul, expressed as she imagined it by coming out of our mouths when we speak? But was she also right to innately be disturbed or confused by the idea that our bodies are dispensable, to be buried like garbage when our departed souls fly free to heaven? Since then I've grown more agitated with the gnostic understandings that many Christians have of humanity and what happens to people when they die. I recently attended a funeral in which the preacher referred to the person's body as a "shell."

Language like this expresses a kind of Christian hyperdualism, one that offers an overweening separation of all of life into two main categories: the sacred and the profane, or the spiritual and the physical. Our souls belong in the sacred category, but our bodies are profane or at best spiritually neutral. Whether they're prepared to admit it or not, many Christians behave as operational hyperdualists. And many preachers reinforce this worldview. They place far greater importance on the spiritual over the physical, and they promote the church's mission as being chiefly concerned with readying souls for heaven and teaching the faithful how to endure their human physical experience. In other words, they value so-called soul work so much over physical life that such physical activities are either demonized (sex, eating), sacralized by being put into service of the church (art, architecture, music) or completely ignored (exercise, work, play). Work, farming, making love, playing with children, picnics, arts and crafts—these things were neither here nor there as far as many people's spirituality is concerned. Overall, most people lead mainly profane lives, with occasional moments of the sacred or transcendent, while they await the day when their departing souls will be freed to the heavenly realms. This kind of thinking naturally leads to the defleshing of the

Christian experience. Excarnate forms of religion are the obvious outworking of hyperdualism. As long as we don't get drunk or have sex with the wrong person, our bodies don't come into the equation. Our faith operates in our heads, not in any meaningful bodily forms.

In understanding Christian hyperdualism it is helpful to see that it is predicated on a number of important differences and distinctions. These are the three main dichotomies worth noting.

1. *Christian anthropological dualism.* This dichotomy is the view that humankind is composed of two separate substances, one being temporal and the other eternal. These substances are usually called "body" and "soul" (or "spirit") respectively. The seventeenth-century French philosopher René Descartes posited that there is a divisible, mechanical body and an indivisible, immaterial mind that interact with one another. The body perceives external inputs, and the awareness of them comes from the soul. He even suggested that the point of interaction between the two is at the pineal gland in the brain. The church went further, influenced by the Platonism of the early church, ascribing differing values to the soul over the body and then going further again by absolutizing the two into a master-slave relationship in which the body is the rebellious slave of the soul and must be ruled as a subject is ruled by the king. We are familiar with idea of ascetic monks flagellating themselves with whips as part of their discipline and devotional practice, and while this practice is considered abhorrent today, the belief that the soul is potentially pure and the body eternally sinful still describes how many Christians view the composition of human nature.

2. *Christian metaphysical dualism.* A further movement in Christian dualistic thought is the metaphysical idea that heaven is of great importance and the earth rather unimportant. In this thinking heaven is the true light, making the earth just a shadow of sorts. We hear this kind of idea spoken of at every Christian funeral

where the officiating minister declares the recently deceased to have slipped from their bondage to this mortal coil and flown free to heaven. This is an absolutized duality, and it naturally results in a morbid obsession with all things otherworldly to the exclusion of anything good or godly in this world. When we do encounter earthly beauty, like a sunrise or a mountain peak, it is a seen as a precursor of the true beauty that we be seen in heaven. This kind of dualism appears in myriad worship songs and hymns, though it's probably best remembered in Sanford Bennett's immortal spiritual *In the Sweet By and By* (1868):

> There's a land that is fairer than day,
> And by faith we can see it afar;
> For the Father waits over the way,
> To prepare us a dwelling place there.

> In the sweet by and by,
> We shall meet on that beautiful shore.

This describes how many Christians see reality.

3. *Christian religious dualism.* This is the particular aspect of dualism I was reacting to in *The Shaping of Things to Come.* It involves the quarantining of religious faith to a small corner of one's life and treating it as an entirely personal, private matter that has little bearing on the majority of daily life. Like a hobby, faith becomes a sideline to everyday life, even if it is an enriching and meaningful one. Sociologists Christian Smith and Melinda Lundquist Denton refer to this as belief in a "moralistic therapeutic deism" and claim that it is the most common form of religious faith among American teenagers.[7]

According to their research Smith and Denton say that young Americans hold to the view that being a good, moral person is important for living a happy life, and belief in God is useful because of the therapeutic benefits he provides to its adherents. Those who hold to moralistic therapeutic deism have a "belief in a particular kind of God: one who exists, created the world, and defines our general moral order, but not one who is particularly personally involved in one's affairs—especially affairs in which one would prefer not to have God involved."[8] They go on to characterize the God of moral therapeutic deism as "something like a combination Divine Butler and Cosmic Therapist: he's always on call, takes care of any problems that arise, professionally helps his people to feel better about themselves, and does not become too personally involved in the process."[9] This kind of dualism describes how many Christians use their faith.

## The Pervasiveness of Dualism

Dualistic views dominate the church today, and I would suggest they dominate societal views as well, contributed to in no small measure by the church's influence over the centuries. Filmgoers are regularly presented with a dualistic worldview in films like *Field of Dreams* (1989), *Ghost* (1990), *Hearts and Souls* (1993) and *What Dreams May Come* (1998), in which the spirits or souls or ghosts (it's never clear if there's a difference) of deceased people hover around their loved ones and attempt to mop up some kind of "unfinished business" on earth before heading off to heaven or the spirit world or wherever. This idea formed the basis of the popular CBS series *The Ghost Whisperer* (2005-2010), which followed the work of Melinda Gordon (Jennifer Love Hewitt), who has the ability to see and communicate with earthbound spirits and help them resolve their problems and cross over into the light or the spirit world.

Over on Syfy (formerly Sci-Fi Channel), John Edward does a similar thing in his program, *Crossing Over*, where he questions audience members based on cryptic or incomplete messages communicated to him by their deceased friends and relatives. Edward says he receives images and clues from "the other side," but that he needs the audience to assist him in interpreting them. Invariably, the message communicated by the deceased ones "crossing over" is one of comfort or affirmation to those they've left behind.

In this highly dualistic world, disembodied spirits have got a lot of work to do before they are free to leave the earth. This idea is mocked somewhat in the Ricky Gervais film *Ghost Town* (2008), in which a misanthropic dentist has a near-death experience and recovers only to be able to see and communicate with the many ghosts who populate the area. The earthbound spirits then proceed to annoy him until he helps them with personal business that was left unfinished when they died. The harried dentist (played by Gervais) is run off his feet attending to their various requests. This is a far cry from the afterlife imagined by talk show host Stephen Colbert, who once told N. T. Wright in an interview, "I always thought heaven would be sitting on the porch forever, drinking mint juleps with Ronald Reagan."

In fact N. T. Wright, in his book about the afterlife, *Surprised by Hope*, outlines the strange concoction of beliefs that comprises modern Western thinking about life and death, and criticizes the disembodied notion of heaven that he contends most evangelicals believe in. According to Wright, evangelicals are dangerously ignoring the doctrinal belief in the Apostles' Creed that affirms "we believe in the resurrection of the body." Illustrating his point regarding belief in the disembodied afterlife so common today, he quotes a tribute to the recently deceased Princess Diana placed outside Buckingham Palace that read (as if in Diana's own breathless voice), "I did not leave you at all. I am still with you. I am in the sun and in the wind. I am even in the rain. I did not die, I am with you all."[10]

We might scoff at these expressions of dualism in society, but the church has played a decisive role in promoting them, both in the way Christendom shaped European/Western thinking and in the everyday ways we talk about our view on life. My casual conversation with my daughter in the graveyard is a case in point. And I've lost count of the number of times, when confronted with the death of a loved one, that Christians have remarked that so-and-so is in a "better place." I was visiting a dying parishioner in the hospital once when the pastor of one of her sons arrived. Chatting with me in the waiting room, the other pastor said, "Betty has been through a lot, hasn't she? If I were her, I would be ready to go. I'm ready to get out of here myself. I'm ready to leave this broken world." I'm not questioning his sincerity or his good intentions or honest care for this woman, but his comment betrays a theological worldview that belittles this world as something nonspiritual, as something that we should be quick to get away from.

No doubt, many people have this view in part because they read the New Testament with dualistic lenses and find passages that seem to indicate that we should have a low view of earth. One such passage is Philippians 1 where Paul says, "For to me, to live is Christ and to die is gain" (v. 21) and "I desire to depart and be with Christ, which is better by far" (v. 23).

I think we can agree with Paul that death is gain because in it we gain Christ in a tangible way—and this *is* what this passage teaches. But for those who read Paul's words through a dualistic lens, this is not how they interpret it: Death is gain for most Christians because *that* life is better than *this* life. *That* reality is better than *this* reality. This betrays their belief that this world has no part in redemption; it is permanently lost. But is that what Paul is saying here? The key question that we have to answer is: why is death *gain* to Paul? Death is gain to Paul not because he thinks that living in the redeemed creation is a bad thing but because he longs to see and be with Christ in a direct, physical sense. These verses do not denigrate earthly life as something bad, rather they prize tangible Christ as something to be desired deeply. This isn't to belittle Christ in any way. In fact, what Paul is saying is that as a Christian he believes the earth, this earthly life and the temporal are all good, but that he would trade them in an instant if it meant gaining Christ in a tangible way. Consider the alternative dualistic interpretation: Paul is saying that the earth, this earthly life and the temporal are all bad, but he would trade them in an instant if it meant gaining Christ in a tangible way. That's not much of a trade. In fact, that interpretation does belittle Christ.

Another example of Christian dualism is the reaction Christians have when they hear preachers or worship leaders talk about the need to worship the Lord in all we do. Christians are usually at a loss when they hear this, and not only because the preacher or the worship leader has just been demonstrating the opposite of what they are saying, but because they can't conceive of what worship looks like in the everyday. They might be wondering whether the worship pastor expects them to lead their coworkers in a worship song in their workplace. A friend of mine, who works for a very large corporation, recently began attending an office Bible study during his lunch break in the hope that by gathering with other believers he would draw strength for living out his faith incarnationally at work. However, the study turned out to be exclusively focused on how they could share their faith with their colleagues. When my friend asked whether they could also draw illumination for their daily work, he was looked at askance. Dualism like this only sees God being present in an evangelistic conversation or a lunchroom Bible study. Because it has relegated worship to only the apparently spiritual side of the equation, it can't understand worshiping God through the *totality* of life. Dualistic thinking has no framework for carrying faith in deeply meaningful bodily forms, whether they be via ritual, liturgy, work, hospitality, play, pastoral care or social action.

What we need is a new framework, an *incarnational* framework, to countermand the excarnate trends and stresses being placed on our lives today. Worshiping God through our work, for example, does not mean bringing those religious things (over there) into our work and daily life (over here). It recognizes that we have only one life, and that who we are does not change from one context or realm to the next, because there is only one context—life. Separating life into two (or more) compartments also tends to foster a faith-works dichotomy that is roundly condemned in the epistle of James, but more on that later.

Dualism is the philosophical foundation of excarnation. It was unhelpful while the church was dominating Western culture, but it is disconcerting now that the West has embraced secularism. In the past, when spirituality or religion was greatly valued, the devaluing of the body worked in the church's favor, but in a post-Christian secular West, where religious practice is devalued, we find ourselves in a time of monumental disenchantment and disillusionment. Nothing is sacred.

Dualism was not part of the Hebraic or ancient Jewish mindset. Whereas the Greeks believed in an incarnated soul—a preexistent soul wrapped in flesh—the Hebrews conceived of an animated body (Genesis 2). In continuity with the Old Testament, the New Testament views humans as a unity rather than dualistically. The most important advance in the New Testament is the belief that the essential personality, whether called the *psyche* or the *pneuma*, survives bodily death. This soul or spirit may be temporarily disembodied, but it is not complete without the body, and its continued existence after bodily death is dependent on God and is not a natural endowment of the soul. What we see in the New Testament is a modified dualism, something similar to what Nancey Murphy has called *spirited bodies*.[11] This is an important consideration to keep in mind. The *body-versus-soul* thinking that dominates much of Christianity today leads us to a devaluing of the body and bodily forms of Christian experience.

The church needs to acknowledge how we've contributed to our present state. But more importantly we need to look for ways to demonstrate to society what spirited-bodies-in-community can look like. We need to re-elevate the spiritual; but equally, we need to elevate the bodily. When Paul yearns to gain Christ in a real and tangible way, he doesn't do so to the exclusion of encountering Christ bodily in this world. Excarnation divides life into two worlds: (1) the ideological world of ideas and fantasy and story and spirituality and religious faith, and (2) the material world of action and work and building and serving and touching and caring. And while minimizing the latter, the Christian community has tacitly or actively affirmed the former as the domain in which God operates. This has significant moral repercussions that invite more incarnational Christian responses.

# 3

# Wandering Aimlessly in
# a Moral Minefield

*As the soul does not live idly in the body,*
*but gives motion and vigor to every member and part,*
*so the Spirit of God cannot dwell in us without*
*manifesting Himself by the outward effects.*

JOHN CALVIN

🔲

**N**owhere is the disconnect between the body and the mind/spirit more apparent in contemporary society than in the area of morality. In our moral framework, excarnation is manifest in such things as the devaluing of the human body, often shown in the widespread use of pornography, a loss of modesty, the emergence of the depiction of graphic violence as a comedic device, a reduction of importance placed on the physical act, and the utilizing of others as objects for our own gain or pleasure. The relatively recent designation "friends with benefits" betrays an assumption that we are entirely materialistic creatures with physical needs that can be easily and conveniently accommodated by others. These days the idea of a metaphysical union between two bodies and souls is considered quaint and romantic. Worse still, the immorality of our age can be assessed by such horrors as human sex trafficking and the trade in human organs, where we see the debasing of the body as a mere commodity at its most obvious.

## OUR ZOMBIE APOCALYPSE

In the first season of Frank Darabont's adaptation of *The Walking Dead* comics, the central character, Sheriff Rick Grimes, emerges from a coma to discover he has survived a zombie apocalypse. Stumbling from his now derelict hospital, he finds his hometown, King County, Georgia, overrun by living dead versions of his neighbors—limping, groaning, bluish pale, veiny monsters who want nothing more than to consume living flesh. Unable to comprehend the awful truth (he has just woken up from a coma, after all), Grimes staggers into the path of the marauding flesh eaters, only to be rescued by Morgan Jones, one of the few remaining King County residents not infected by the zombie-creating virus.

Jones has barricaded himself and his young son, Duane, in their family's home, and despite the dire conditions, he still endeavors to create some form of normality for Duane. He reads him storybooks, continues to correct his grammar and even insists on mealtime prayers. They have learned how to avoid the zombies when they forage for food and water, and they have blackened their windows to avoid detection at night. The Joneses take the stricken Rick Grimes into this bizarre attempt at suburban life surrounded by chaos and death. A metaphor for the bunkered existence of suburbia, perhaps?

While sheltering with Morgan and Duane, Rick learns that Morgan's wife, Jenny, had herself been infected by a zombie bite, and instead of administering the *coup de grace*, Morgan decided to let her go outside to wander with the other zombies. This is a decision that continues to haunt him. After bringing Rick up to speed on the ins and outs of surviving a zombie holocaust, he seems to re-alize afresh that his decision to allow Jenny to wander lifelessly as one of the living dead was a mistake. Later that night Morgan tucks Duane into bed and tells him to read his comic books (what else?). Morgan then goes upstairs and flicks through the family's photo albums to select a picture of Jenny, which he sticks it to the window frame. In the gloaming of a mid-summer evening, he then aims his rifle into the street below, and after shooting a couple of other zombies to lure his wife out, he trains his sights on her, his gaze shifting from the photo of her beautiful smiling face to the gruesome image of her caught in the crosshairs. And yet he still cannot bring himself to kill her. He tries to steel himself against his emotions several more times, yet each fails in kind. Morgan's love for Jenny means he is unable to kill her even when he knows her "spirit" has gone and it's only her physical shell left wandering the streets.

Okay, I know zombies aren't real, but the current obsession with them in popular culture is intriguing. *The Walking Dead* has been a smash hit television series, and Mila Jovovich's relentlessly bad *Resident Evil* zombie holocaust franchise—up to five films and counting—has collectively scooped over $700 million in ticket sales worldwide. Even megastar Brad Pitt has got in on the act with his big budget zombie thriller, *World War Z*.

But if cheap thrills are all there is to a zombie movie, why are they so popular and so enduring as a pop culture device? Some have suggested that a zombie apocalypse is a more palatable end-of-the-world scenario because it's a truly secular one with no judgmental deities presiding over the fate of humankind. Others have specu-lated that it's a cracked, secular version of resurrection. However, culture watcher Dan Birlew suggests the reasons for the popularity of zombie fiction lies somewhere more primal:

There's an entire world full of walking punching bags. People are now zombies, and you have to kill them before they kill you. So it doesn't really matter what you do to them, because they're not people anymore. They're former people that you can beat down and tear apart in the most gruesome ways you can think of. The more clever and savage, the better. Take out all your frustrations in all the ways you ever dreamed, it doesn't matter anymore. No one's going to stop you from killing a monster, even if it used to be a person. . . . Perhaps swinging on a guy's head with a cricket bat is starting to sound like a good way to blow off some steam. But the only problem is, you're talking about a person. So you need something that's not a person, but a kind of rudimentary semi-person with no intelligence. That's what a zombie is, that's what role it fulfills. And if that's the case, swing away.[1]

In various zombie films the undead are dispatched by gunshots and crowbar blows to the head, by being run over by cars, scorched with flamethrowers, attacked by chainsaws and clobbered by metal skillets. And if screen depictions don't offer enough ideas, goofy websites like *Cracked* offer insightful articles like "Awesome Ways to Kill Zombies!!!" which starts with the three indisputable rules of zombie killing:

1. Killing zombies is a duty of every human being.

2. It is also fun.

3. If you have been able to mix your duty and your fun together, then you must be awesome.[2]

All of which brings me back to Morgan Jones and his zombie wife, Jenny. Why can't he (re)kill her? Why can't he, to take Birlew's point, *swing away at her*? According to the zombie handbook, she's not a person anymore, so shooting her shouldn't be so difficult. But

writer and director Frank Darabont, known for his deeply senti-
mental feature films (*Shawshank Redemption, The Green Mile*), can't
allow Morgan to be so callous. It's a tender moment in a television
series otherwise filled with the kind of cathartic violence so celebrated by Birlew. I suspect that Darabont knows *The Walking Dead*
appeals to those most base yearnings, particularly in young male
viewers, to be completely and wantonly irresponsible in one's
treatment of others.

It's juvenile, testosterone-soaked nonsense, but it reinforces the
point that zombie pictures are trying to appeal to the lust for socially
acceptable wanton bloodshed. Darabont's inclusion of the scene featuring Morgan Jones subverts all the lunacy and mayhem. It reminds
us that actually, deep down, we know that our bodies are precious,
they're not just shells that carry our real selves. Morgan loves Jenny,
and that means he loves the physical manifestation of her, no matter
how diminished it might be, not just her personality that has left her.
If, like all horror genres, zombies represent our deepest fears, then
surely they represent the horror above horrors that we dare not truly
consider, that our bodies might actually be worthless.

## THE FEAR OF THE WORTHLESSNESS OF OUR BODIES

The theory goes that the subjects of horror fiction are personifica-
tions of society's gravest fears, and that as those fears have changed
over time, so have our depictions of them. Consider the vampire,
for example. In their earliest incarnations in medieval times, vampires were ugly, ghoulish creatures of the night, with translucent
skin and long, bony hands and oversized fangs. They served as the
personification of all that Europeans feared in nature. But by the
nineteenth and twentieth centuries human societies were subduing
nature and had found explanations for most natural mysteries and
cures for many common diseases. In this period vampires change
from vile little monsters into suave aristocrats. Enter the white,

European, aristocratic, vampire norm of Count Dracula, Barnabas Collins and Lestat de Lioncourt (to be later played by Tom Cruise). As independently wealthy counts, living in massive castles and emerging at night to suck the blood from poor working-class people, they represented people's fear of the reemergence of a godless aristocracy. More recently, vampires are good-looking teenagers. In *The Lost Boys*, teenage vampires run rampant in sunny California with the tag line: "Sleep all day. Party all night. Never grow old. Never die. It's fun to be a vampire." The same is true of *The Vampire Diaries* and the *Twilight* series.

So, do rampant adolescents represent our greatest fears today? Well, if you look at the vampire metaphor from the perspective of postmodern theory, it gets more interesting. Postmodernism totally subverts the whole in-out oppositional structure of modernism, so some postmodernists say that a key to understanding the vampire is that it is itself an inherently deconstructive figure: the monster used to be human, the undead used to be alive, the monster looks like us. And when you think about it, nothing deconstructs that in-out, black-white dichotomy more than fresh-faced beautiful young people actually being the bloodthirsty undead.

But back to zombies. Dispatching them casually and relentlessly, though at one level highly entertaining for some people, is horrifying because it too represents our greatest fear: that we are dispensable. While many people are happy to treat their own bodies and those of other people like zombies—casually and indiscriminately—deeper down there's a sense of horror that our bodies could mean so little. Action films like the *Rambo* or the *Die Hard* series, in which scores of bad guys (whether Muslim extremists or a megalomaniac's henchmen) are slaughtered in droves, have become politically incorrect these days, so we've had to resort to killing unhuman objects like zombies for the same thrill effect. And all the while we are picking at the scab of our nagging anxiety of our own dispensability.

This warped desire to see human bodies humiliated while at the same time being disturbed by it plays itself out in our societal obsession with online pornography. Studies report that there has been a shift away from the comically contrived scenarios, for which blue movies were once infamous, to darker films where the performers are filmed in debasing and humiliating situations. Apparently, a popular porn subgenre is the filming of performers having sex in public places while bystanders watch. It's not enough to know that you're part of a virtual audience watching a sex act on a screen, you need to watch an audience observing the act as well. Is there anything more zombie-like than watching bystanders watch a couple having sex in a store or a public park? It might be as titillating and entertaining as clobbering zombies, but it's also as depraved and demeaning. But these are real people, not actors with fake blood and a bad gait. Surely, this is the depth of excarnation. It is as soulless a physical act as you can imagine. Sure, we're titillated, but we're also sickened by it.

## The Weight of Productivity

Of course, you might not be into porn or zombie films, but these, like the tip of an iceberg, are simply examples of how our deep fears or longings breach the surface via pop culture. Under the murky waters our society has embraced a form of morality completely shaped by excarnate realities. The idea that our bodies are without intrinsic worth is at the root of the highly industrialized understanding of human value. When we abandon the biblical idea that people are begotten and assume that human bodies have no intrinsic worth, then the only value we can ascribe to them is the value our bodies are capable of generating. We make ourselves valuable, constructing our own worth by our own individual wills and by the institutions of society that need the services we can provide. In such a highly industrialized society human beings are rendered as tools and valued for their capacity and output. For this reason the elderly or those with a disability are treated differently than the able-bodied whose worth is greater to us. Catholic theologian Oliver O'Donovan summarizes this in his classic book *Begotten or Made*:

> What marks this culture out most importantly is not anything that it does, but what it thinks. It is not "technological" because its instruments of making are extraordinarily sophisticated (though that is evidently the case), but because it thinks of everything it does as a form of instrumental making. Politics (which should surely be the most non-instrumental of activities) is talked of as "making a better world"; love is "building a successful relationship." There is no place for simply doing. The fate of a society which sees, wherever it looks, nothing but the products of the human will, is that it fails, when it does see some aspect of human activity which is not a matter of construction, to recognize the significance of what it sees and to think about it appropriately. This blindness in the realm of thought is the heart of what it is to be a technological culture.[3]

I would contend that all contemporary anxieties hang on this analysis. If sex isn't producing something, it is seen as valueless, or its value is converted into pornography or prostitution and sold to the highest bidders. Everything must bear the weight of productivity. And if you start there, the arguments change, becoming less about the morality of pornography or violent films or gambling or anything else, and more about the anthropology that undergirds our technological development and whether, and how far, we ought to protect anything natural from our technocratic intrusions. This is a form of the disengagement and objectification we looked at in chapter two, and the spiritual climate it produces is a culture of individualism, narcissism, materialism and triviality. In such an ex-carnate environment it is easy to objectivize others, rank feelings above morals, prefer the therapeutic above the transcendent and nonconformity over authority, and absolute freedom becomes an intense form of slavery.

If we were meant to subjugate nature by disengagement and ob-jectification, then it follows that eventually we would come to be-lieve that we must do likewise to our own natural bodies. Human beings' control of nature by the subjugation of both body and earth to the rational powers of the mind has been a dominant theme of modern Western culture. To act as an industrious and rational person the passions and physical limitations of the body must be "brought under control." We might no longer express our view of our body as a source of evil and a hindrance to our achievement of virtue, but we still see it as inferior to the spirit or mind, as an object we must bring under rational control. After all, we use our rational power to improve nature, to bring water to the desert and invent vaccinations, then it follows we will do likewise to develop ways of altering our bodies to have unnatural characteristics we find pro-ductive. This might be as seemingly innocent as taking pills to sleep and gulping Red Bull to stay awake. But none of it is really that innocent after all. It is an expression of the disconnection we have with our bodies. We use them. We are rarely at one with them.

In this way of thinking the body is perceived as confinement and limitation. Therefore, we must disengage from it in order to control it for greater capacity and value. Anorexia nervosa is just one man-ifestation of our modernist drive to exercise rational, mental control-mastery over body and nature, as are porn stars' breast aug-mentations and sport stars' use of steroids. Our bodies must be shaped and stimulated in order to gain maximum use from them, not in order to exercise self-care. For example, this excarnate ethic of control affects women's attitudes toward menstruation, a physical aspect of themselves that is, biologically speaking, as involuntary as breathing and blinking, and yet in a recent study 69 percent of the women said that given the choice, they would rather not menstruate.[4] Companies that advertise feminine products routinely appeal to women's desire to be freed from the inconvenience of menstruation in order to be able to work, swim or cavort on the beach. Menstruation can't be celebrated as a monthly reminder of the capacity of the female body to reproduce life. Women can't be encouraged to be at one with their bodies. Rather, their pesky or annoying bodies must be controlled so they can be more productive. Feminist author Penelope Washbourn writes,

> To be limited by our bodies, whether in sickness or death, or particularly by the female body processes, is considered weakness and threatens our "normal" forms of mastery and self-control. We try to overcome fatigue or pain with drugs and stimulants and fail to accept our bodies as part of an ongoing life process which has its own rhythms. To regard menstruation primarily as an unfortunate nuisance that now can be handled largely through better sanitary products is to treat female sexuality as an unfortunate burden or weakness which can to a large extent be overcome and thus ignored.[5]

## I AM MY BODY

To be fully present in our bodies, to inhabit flesh and to be at home in the world where God has placed us is a difficult task, particularly for Christians who have for so long been taught to yearn for a home in the age to come. We have for so long been presented with a form of hyperdualism that encourages us to be ambivalent about our bodies and to believe God is not of this world and neither should we be. But holding out hope for a new age shouldn't mean we cannot be at peace with our bodies in this age. Our attitude should be more like Paul's, who rejoices in his capacity to glorify God in his body, while also hoping for the new heaven and the new earth. To the Philippians he writes,

> I eagerly expect and hope that I will in no way be ashamed, but will have sufficient courage so that now as always Christ will be exalted in my body, whether by life or by death. For to me, to live is Christ and to die is gain. If I am to go on living in the body, this will mean fruitful labor for me. Yet what shall I choose? I do not know! I am torn between the two. (Philippians 1:20-23)

To live is Christ. This is a well-worn biblical expression. But it doesn't simply refer to one man's personal piety. It has significant moral implications. To go on living in this body not only means fruitful labor, as Paul points out, it also means acknowledging that the bodies of others deserve equal status and respect. If I can glorify Christ in my body—whether by a fruitful life or by death—the body is a legitimate space, indeed, a sacred space. And we know this intuitively even though we do our best to disassociate ourselves from physical pain, menstruation or perceived physical defects. We *are* our bodies. We don't live *in* our bodies. And therefore our bodies and the bodies of others are precious and worthy of respect. Kenneth Bailey says,

> We are not disembodied spirits. Nor are we souls temporarily imprisoned in a body that one day will be stripped away as we return to pure spirit. Death itself is conquered by the resurrection of the *body*, affirmed Paul (1 Cor 15:42-50), not through the transmigration of the soul. Furthermore, Paul called this new body a "spiritual body."[6]

This has monumental moral implications. Recently, a leaky Indonesian fishing boat full of asylum seekers from Afghanistan sank in the Timor Sea as it made its way to seek refuge in Australia. The Australian navy was dispatched to effect a rescue, but it arrived too late. As they approached the wreckage of the boat, news came of another vessel loaded with refugees also in distress not far away. The naval ship was forced to turn away from recovering the bodies of the drowned Afghanis to rescue others in grave difficulty on the high seas. This story had significant impact in Australia, where a public debate raged about the morality of leaving corpses floating in the sea. Some felt that even if the naval vessel could have reached the bodies it was not their business to recover anonymous refugees lost at sea. Others insisted it is a fundamentally human quality to show respect for the bodies of the dead.

It is believed that even the Neanderthals buried their dead. For the Egyptians the rituals associated with the preservation of the body ensured a smooth passage to the afterlife. Are there more extraordinary monuments to the human regard for the dead body than the tombs of the Pharaohs—those great prisms of light on the plains of Giza?

The Romans and Greeks were aghast at the thought of an unburied body, but they regarded death and the dead with horror, not hope. For them proper treatment of the body was necessary to release the soul from its fleshy prison. There's that horrible scene you might recall from the Iliad where Achilles drags the body of Hector around the walls of Troy from his chariot as a sign of his utter contempt for the Trojans. He rubs their noses in the taboo.

For the Jews a dead body was unclean and untouchable (Numbers 19:16), which was ironically a way of ensuring the body of the dead person was treated with great care by the living. It was thought a great curse to have one's body lie unburied and exposed to the ravages of the wild animals. Consequently, the women who came to anoint Jesus' body in the tomb were treating him with reverence and tenderness.

This makes Jesus' insistence on touching the dead bodies of Jairus's daughter and his friend Lazarus quite astounding. Jesus did not fear the dead, and they did not contaminate him. His own bodily resurrection from the dead signaled the Christian hope for the ongoing identity of a person with his or her own body. The body is not a prison to be released from but *is* the person in a profound sense. If the church is to have any hope of truly embracing the challenge of incarnational mission, we will be required to embrace an embodied sense of ourselves, to respect our fleshly existence, not as a putrid interim arrangement but as intrinsic to who we are as God's people. Furthermore, we will need to be freed from the inclination to treat others as zombies, as no-things, as worthless, and embrace an ethic of love for all.

# 4

# The Moral Ambiguity of Our Time

*Waste no more time arguing about what
a good [person] should be. Be one.*

MARCUS AURELIUS

The objectification of the human body is one of the primary effects of the technological society, and yet rarely do we hear the church speak up about this topic. Certainly, there are calls from the church to resist the use of pornography, and of course there is also the pro-life stance adopted by Christians. These calls are often based on an interest in holiness, sexual fidelity and the sanctity of life. But I often wonder why the church isn't as equally concerned about the sanctity of the human body when we have a utilitarian view of our own bodies and the bodies of others. When did you last hear the church speak out about the excarnate sensibilities of tampon commercials or zombie movies? When does the church affirm the created goodness of our bodies or celebrate them? For that matter, when does the church side with the labor movement to argue that workers cannot be treated as utilities and be discarded when no longer useful?

One of the most powerful moments of the civil rights movement was the image of over two hundred striking sanitation workers marching through Memphis in 1968, despite martial law and the presence of four thousand National Guard troops, carrying placards that read "I Am a Man." It was a poignant call to be viewed as a complete person, not just a tool for collecting garbage. It was a protest against the excarnate impulses of racism. That night in Memphis, indeed his last night on earth, Martin Luther King Jr. told a church filled with sanitation workers, "We've got to give ourselves to this struggle until the end. Nothing would be more tragic than to stop at this point in Memphis. We've got to see it through."[1] Where are the Martin Luther Kings of today? The people of God should have a keener sense of outrage when we see people being treated as objects for use by others for their gain or pleasure.

The emergence of a growing outrage about human sex trafficking is a sign that things are changing, but the sex trafficking industry continues on unabated. Now, we hear of the unconscionable illegal trade in human organs around the world. In fact, in 2012 the World Health Organization warned of an alarming rise in the trade, saying that around 10 percent of transplant procedures involve organs that have been purchased on the black market. Organ traffickers are exploiting the poor in such places as China, India and Pakistan to cash in on the rising international demand for replacement kidneys. Western patients can pay up to $200,000 for a kidney, while the poor who sell their organ receive around $5,000, at most. Stories are told of people being offered an iPad for a kidney. In one tragic story, a man swapped an eye for an ice cart, imagining it would lead to a new life for his family. But because of his poor commercial acumen his ice carting business went broke within six months, leaving him jobless and eyeless. In Western countries in close proximity to Southeast Asia, like Australia, there is growing evidence that donors are being flown into the country to have their organs harvested under Western medical conditions, not for the benefit of the donor but for the safeguard of the $200,000 kidney for the purchaser. Of course, the human organ trade is illegal, but with such incredible profits to be made, and with such a desperate need for organ transplants among wealthy Westerners, the temptation to see human bodies as commodities is too great.

In the intriguing (and confusing) action thriller film *Source Code*, soldier Coulter Stevens (Jake Gyllenhaal) wakes up in the body of an unknown man and discovers he's part of a mission to find the bomber of a Chicago commuter train. It transpires that Stevens has suffered unspeakable injuries on the battlefront and that he is basically a brain in a jar kept in a military hospital and being used by brilliant but amoral scientists. They send him into something called the "source code," where he gets to inhabit the last eight minutes of the life of Sean Fentress, one of the commuters on the doomed train. By reliving those last eight minutes over and over, he is able to search for clues to the bomber's identity so he can relay the information to his scientist controllers and the bomber can be caught.

Eventually, Stevens/Fentress succeeds in his mission, but then begs his superior, Colleen Goodwin (Vera Farmiga), to send him back into the source code one last time in an attempt to save the passengers on the train by disarming the bomb, capturing the bomber and turning him into the authorities. Colter wants to do this despite the fact that source code creator Dr. Rutledge (Jeffrey Wright) has told him it's futile as he only has the last eight minutes of Sean Fentress's life to live. After all, Fentress became toast when the bomb originally exploded. Based on that logic, there's nothing Colter can do but relive the eight minutes all over again, save the train or not, and return back to the film's narrative reality. Despite his request being denied by Rutledge, Colleen goes against orders and sends Colter in one last time. This time he disarms the bomb, captures the bomber and—this bit is important—sends Colleen a text message letting her know a crisis has been averted and the source code works. Time seems to stand still as the eight minutes allotted to him are up. At that moment, in the real world, Colleen terminates Colter's life by switching off his life support. The film then switches back to Colter in the source code where time resumes, he gets off the train with Fentress's girlfriend, Christina (Michelle Monaghan) and they live happily ever after.

The evil scientists are routed and the beautiful couple rides off into the sunset. Except that the so-called happy ending is based on a very morally dubious premise.

If we're meant to believe that Stevens is enjoying a whole new life in a real world, then we have to believe that in order for Colter to be alive, Sean Fentress, the man whose body he's been borrowing for his eight-minute quantum leaps, is now dead, erased by the overwriting of Colter's consciousness. Is that right? Is that moral? Is the life of one innocent man who was given no choice in the matter a fair price to pay for the lives of many other innocents? In an excarnate world, where our identity is separate from our bodies, it certainly is.

If you've seen the film, you might be thinking that maybe Colter is just dreaming about a great life from his new home in the brain jar. Except, it *must* be a real alternative world. It cannot simply be a shadow of reality, as Jeffrey Wright's scientist insists once Colter starts questioning things. So, isn't there something very disturbing about the entire premise? If the plan is, in effect, to put Colter Stevens into the last eight minutes of memories of Sean Fentress and to allow him to construct an entire alternate world from these memories, then the morality of the piece is based on the assumption that an innocent man has to die so that Colter Stevens can live. Fentress's body is an object to be used by the heroic Colter for his and others' gain. There's nothing quite as creepy as that, and yet films like this, based on so dubious a moral foundation, are ignored by the church. Perhaps it's the excarnate nature of the church that

has numbed our ability to sense the moral ambiguity of entertainment like this.

Just as pervasive is the impact of media violence on society, in
particular on young children and adolescents. Nothing leads to the
dehumanizing of others quite like thousands of hours of violent
video games and films. The nature and level of that impact was first
questioned after the spate of high school shootings in the late 1990s
and early 2000s, in which many of the perpetrators were reported to
have been fans of violent video games like *Doom* and *Counter-Strike*.
Now, a growing body of evidence, including reports by the Surgeon
General, the American Psychological Association and the National
Institute of Mental Health, points to the conclusion that exposure to
violence in the media may indeed make a person more accepting of
it. The American Academy of Pediatrics estimates young people will
view 200,000 acts of violence on television by the time they're
eighteen, including 16,000 murders, and studies have found that
more than 85 percent of video games contain violence. Even children's cartoons may contain up to twenty acts of violence per hour.
Furthermore, 69 percent of men depicted on television are involved
in violence; 11 percent are killers. Making conclusive links between
the viewing of violent images and the conduct of violent behavior is
difficult, although a Canadian study documented a 160 percent increase in aggression, hitting, shoving and biting in first- and second-
grade students after TV was first introduced in 1973, with no change
in behavior in children in two control communities.[2] According to
the American Medical Association, fifteen years after the introduction
of television, homicides, rapes and assaults doubled in the United
States. Twenty percent of suburban high schoolers endorse shooting
someone "who has stolen something from you." In the United States,
approximately two million teenagers carry knives, guns, clubs or
razors, with as many as 135,000 taking them to school.[3]

Another study conducted by psychologists from Iowa State University involving college students revealed that subjects who were asked to play violent video games showed lower heart rates and skin responses after subsequently watching footage of people being beaten, stabbed and shot than did students who were asked to play nonviolent games. The psychologists hypothesized that violent video games may lead people to get used to violence and become physiologically numb to it.[4]

This was something known to the US military and has been openly utilized in desensitizing new recruits for decades. By 1946, the US Army began pioneering a change in combat training that eventually replaced firing at bull's-eye targets with realistic, man-shaped, pop-up targets that fall when hit. Psychologists know that this kind of operant conditioning will reliably influence the primitive, midbrain processing of a frightened human being, just as fire drills condition terrified school children to respond properly during a fire, and repetitious stimulus-response conditioning in flight simulators enables frightened pilots to respond reflexively to emergency situations. Dave Grossman, in his book *On Killing*, refers to his own military training:

> From the moment you step off the bus you are physically and verbally abused: countless pushups, endless hours at attention or running with heavy loads, while carefully trained professionals take turns screaming at you. Your head is shaved, you are herded together naked and dressed alike, losing all individuality. This brutalization is designed to break down your existing mores and norms, and to accept a new set of values that embrace destruction, violence, and death as a way of life. In the end, you are desensitized to violence and accept it as a normal and essential survival skill in your brutal new world.[5]

If this ambiguity isn't disturbing enough in the morally treacherous world of combat, it is increasing seeping into the excarnate world we live in. The human body is being reckoned less and less human. It is a commodity, dispensable and replaceable when considered worthless. The excarnate world is one that measures worth only in widgets, numbers and quantities. It has almost completely abandoned the idea that human beings transcend processes and are made for relationality and wisdom, not merely productivity. While your kid is playing *Halo* or watching porn or zombie movies, he or she is not attempting to answer the question of what it means to be truly human. While surely that is the task of any civilization, it is ultimately the task of the church. One of the simplest definitions of the mission of God's people that I've heard is "to teach the world a new way to be human." This is what Jesus came to do and what his followers are commanded to model. The civilizing effect of Christianity is not to export Western cultural mores around the world but to catalyze the ongoing effort of a culture or society to answer the question of what it means to be human. The great medical missionary Albert Schweitzer said,

> To be civilized means approximately this: that in spite of the conditions of modern civilization, we remain human. Only the most careful concern for everything which belongs to true human nature can preserve us, amid the conditions of the most advanced external civilization, from going astray from civilization itself. It is only if the longing to become again truly human is kindled in the man of today, that he will be able to find his way out of the confusion in which, blinded by the conceit at his knowledge and pride in his powers, he is at present wandering.[6]

Kindling the longing to be human again. That is our task and challenge. And when it is pursued to its ultimate end, as we will see later, it leads us to relationship with God.

### SUBJECT-OBJECT RELATIONSHIPS

Writing around the same time as Schweitzer, Jewish philosopher Martin Buber explored these themes in his landmark book *I and Thou* (*Ich und Du*), in which he argued that human existence may be defined by the way we engage in dialogue with each other, with the world and with God.[7] The book describes how personal dialogue in those three spheres can define the nature of reality. According to Buber, we adopt one of two attitudes toward the world: I-Thou or I-It. I-Thou is a relation of subject to subject, while I-It is a relation of subject to object. In the I-Thou relationship, humans are aware of each other as having a unity of being. In the I-Thou relationship, humans do not perceive each other as consisting of specific, isolated qualities, but engage in a dialogue involving each other's whole being. In the I-It relationship, on the other hand, humans perceive each other as consisting of specific, isolated qualities, and view themselves as part of a world which consists of things. I-Thou is a relationship of mutuality and reciprocity, while I-It is a relationship of separateness and detachment.

Malcolm Muggeridge told the story of the time when, as a young man living in India, he spied the silhouette of a woman bathing in a stream in the early evening. In the fading light she looked ravishing, and as a lusty young fellow Muggeridge convinced himself she wanted him. He waded through the stream toward her only to realize as he came upon her that the naked woman was wracked with leprosy. She was wrinkled and toothless, her feet deformed, her eye sockets eroded, her fingers but stumps. Muggeridge was so repulsed he fell back into the river and allowed the current to draw him away. Later he wrote that what really shocked him was not the condition of the woman but his own dark appetites that overpowered his feeble will. He wrote, "If only I could paint, I'd make a wonderful picture of a passionate boy running after that and call it: 'The lusts of the flesh.'"[8] As he entered the stream he had con-

vinced himself that the seductive silhouette of the woman was
drawing him, but as he left the river he realized it was dark forces
within him that had propelled him. It was the horror of his I-It relations with his world that shocked him so.

I-It, or subject-object, relationships are highly mechanistic ones.
In *Source Code* Dr. Rutledge uses Colter Stevens, who in turn uses
Sean Fentress, and on it goes. If the church is to be a genuine alternative to the excarnate world around us, we need to learn how to
foster genuine I-Thou relations among our members and between
our members and God. We must invite our members to be as hor-
rified by I-It relations as was young Malcolm Muggeridge emerging
from that Indian stream. According to Buber, God is the eternal Thou
who sustains our relationship to him. In the I-Thou relation between
an individual and God, there is a unity of being in which the individual can always find God. In the I-Thou relation there is no barrier
of other relations that separate the individual from God, and thus the
individual can speak directly to God. This makes sense of both Jesus'
and Paul's emphases on love as the central Christian value. Love, as
a relation between I and Thou, is a subject-to-subject relation in
which I and Thou share a sense of caring, respect, commitment and
responsibility. In the I-It relation the being of the I belongs to I, but
not to It. I-Thou is a relation in which I and Thou have a shared reality. Indeed, the more that the I and Thou share their reality, the
more complete is their reality. Buber contends that the I-Thou relation between the individual and God is a universal relation that is
the foundation for all other relations. In fact, the more one enters into
an I-Thou relationship with God, the more likely they are to affect
such a relationship with others. This is why Martin Luther King Jr.
said to the Memphis sanitation workers, "We've *got to* give ourselves
to this struggle." His I-Thou relation with God propelled him into
such a relation with the poorest and most disregarded people in town.
Is this true for Christian people today?

## On Sinning in Your Heart

One of the justifications for making moral choices in a hyperdual-istic way comes from a misreading of Jesus' words in Matthew 5:27-28 where he counsels his listeners against sinning in their hearts: "You have heard that it was said, 'You shall not commit adultery.' But I tell you that anyone who looks at a woman lustfully has already committed adultery with her *in his heart.*" It should be noted that in the original language, Jesus' term for looking at a woman lustfully means to *keep looking* at her. It has the effect of gazing or staring at a woman with the view to possess her, to use her for one's own pleasure. Jesus is condemning our inclination to treat someone as an object and use them for our own purposes. But is the intent really as bad as actually doing something? Here we see Jesus' moral vision being expressed in the most incarnate fashion. He's saying that we can't separate the spirit from the body and say it's okay to sin inwardly as long as you don't act on it outwardly. He is inviting his listeners to see that lust affects the mind (or the imagination) and the body equally. In fact, he was reacting against the pharisaic attitude that allowed a person to imagine the most debauched sin or to harbor the most intense hatred for someone, but as long as the person didn't act on those feelings he or she was sinless. No, says Jesus, we can't bifurcate human nature into two mutually exclusive zones where a person can sin like there's no tomorrow in one, but be as pure as the driven snow in the other.

There's a question in the Talmud that goes something like this: if two men happen upon a fellow Jew begging for alms and one looks upon him with contempt and aversion, and scoffs at him for his laziness but gives him five shekels, while the other is deeply moved by the beggar's plight, his eyes welling with tears of compassion, but gives him one shekel, who has loved the beggar most? The answer is that the man who gave the most money loved the beggar the most. This is to say, in a Jewish worldview, feelings are fine, but we sin or we love by our actions, not our sentiments. In this way, Paul can claim, when writing to the Philippians, that "as for righteousness based on the law, [I was] faultless" (Philippians 3:6). That is, says Paul, with supreme discipline it was possible to keep the letter of the Jewish law. A person could technically get through life without murdering someone or stealing something or without breaking the sabbath and so on. But when he factored in Jesus' teaching in Matthew 5 about hate being as sinful as murder or lustful fantasies being as sinful as adultery, Paul was also very much aware of how far short he fell. To the Galatians he points out that the law of Moses was not given so clever Pharisees could work out ways to reduce it in order to get around it. The law of Moses was given as a yardstick, a measure for our brokenness and our need for God's grace. As the great British novelist Graham Greene once said, "I had to find a religion to measure my evil against."[9] The law measures our actions, but it also measures our hearts. They are one. This is Jesus' point in the Beatitudes. To detach our actions from our motives leads only to self-righteousness, the sin Paul was only too keenly aware of. But keep in mind that Paul's discussion of the law with the Galatians is couched in an overarching consideration of freedom and grace. Being measured in this way was no terrible thing for Paul (or for Graham Greene, for that matter) because it renewed his appreciation of God's great grace.

In this way, the religion of Paul is such that we see ourselves holistically as *spirited bodies* and therefore that we acknowledge our sin holistically and subsequently experience God's grace equally holistically. In the worldview of Jesus there was no distinction between "inner" or "outer" behavior, and the law was a yardstick measuring our totality as fallen human beings. In another example, note Paul's argument to the Corinthians regarding sexual propriety. He uses an argument that would hardly wash in this day: "Do you not know that your bodies are temples of the Holy Spirit, who is in you, whom you have received from God?" (1 Corinthians 6:19). The argument is predicated on the assumption that his readers acknowledge the holiness of religious buildings. Can this be assumed today? Maybe our parents or grandparents can remember a time when a cathedral or church building was viewed as a sanctuary set apart for the work of the Lord. In their day when a person stepped inside one, he immediately removed his hat. That generation taught their children not to be boisterous or frivolous in the church building for it was the house where they met with God, and so reverent behavior was called for within its precincts. They heard Paul's argument that our body is the sanctuary of the Holy Spirit in a similar way to his original Corinthian readers. But today our bodies are not reverenced in this fashion and in many cases neither are religious buildings. I don't share this to suggest that Paul's argument is invalid. I want to affirm its good sense and agree with the idea of treating our bodies and our spirits as if they are both being made holy by the Spirit of God. My point is that the current generation would not make the same assumptions as Paul here. They see buildings as neutral objects and bodies as commodities with differing values.

This is what we're up against in this secular age. Secularism has reduced reason to scientific objectivity and embraces the highly individualistic Western understanding of the human self. This has led to the bifurcation of faith and reason, of science and religion, of fact and value, and pushed religion and morality to some outlying sphere of subjective opinion. Morality isn't viewed as part of the so-called real world of facts, things we can calculate and manipulate. As Jens Zimmerman says,

> Religious truth is what you merely *believe*; scientific truth is what you *know* because everyone can know it and access it in the same way. From this distinction stems the division of our

society into a secular public realm of administration, law and education on the one hand, and a private realm of religious practices and symbols on the other. Since questions of ultimate purpose and meaning inevitably require religious language, this reductive view of reason excludes them by definition from rational discussion.[10]

By excluding them, we effectively allow ourselves to be marginalized from the great moral discussions of society. This wasn't Jesus' vision for human society. Morality is an entirely social matter, but it's also an entirely personal one. Our feelings cannot be quarantined from the matter. I am my body *and* my mind, and when I allow them to operate in very different ways, very different spheres, I am in great moral danger, and so are those around me. Excarnational impulses are pulling us in this direction, and those who take Jesus' teaching seriously need to work hard to resist them.

# 5

# Religion as an Embodied Experience

*If you want to know what a person
believes, watch what they do.*

BRENNAN MANNING

---

**A**uthor David Wallace Foster had a real thing for sacred moments in sport, particularly those demonstrated by his sporting hero, Swiss tennis star Roger Federer. In a *New York Times Magazine* article titled "Federer as a Religious Experience," he worships at his master's feet:

> If you've never seen the young man play live, then do, in person, on the sacred grass of Wimbledon, through literally withering heat and then wind and rain of the '06 fortnight, then you are apt to have what one of the tournament bus drivers describes as a "bloody near-religious experience." It may be more tempting, at first, to hear a phrase like this as just one more of the overheated tropes that people resort to. . . . But the driver's phrase turns out to be true—literally, for an instant ecstatically—though it takes some time and serious watching to see this truth emerge.[1]

Many of us have probably seen Roger Federer play on television and completely missed the metaphysical sacredness of it. That's because, as Wallace says, we need to engage in the spectacle live, in person, on the court itself, whether the sacred grass of Wimbledon or elsewhere. Those of you who have attended a Grand Slam tennis event, as I have, will know that legendary players like Federer attract enormous crowds, even when they are playing on the outside courts. Everyone wants to be able to say they saw the legend playing live. But why? What is the attraction to the experience of being physically present at a game or concert or event, when a television broadcast often shows more of the action?

Another novelist, Don DeLillo, provides an answer of sorts in the prologue to his monumental novel *Underworld*, where he takes his readers to the final game of the 1951 National League competition between the New York Giants and the Brooklyn Dodgers at the Giants' home-field Polo Grounds, the game during which Bobby Thomson hit the so-called "Shot Heard 'Round the World'" in the ninth inning to capture the pennant. In a side note DeLillo describes Russ Hodges, the voice of the Giants who broadcasts the games for WMCA, looking out over the field during a lull in the game.

> But he finds himself thinking of the time his father took him to see Dempsey fight Willard in Toledo and what a thing that was, what a measure of the awesome, the Fourth of July and a hundred and ten degrees and a crowd of shirtsleeved men in straw hats, many wearing handkerchiefs spread beneath their hats and down to their shoulders, making them look like play-Arabs, and the greatness of the beating big Jess took in that white hot ring, the way the sweat and blood came misting off his face every time Dempsey hit him. When you see a thing like that, a thing that becomes a newsreel, you begin to feel you are a carrier of some solemn scrap of history.[2]

As good a writer as he is (and he's a great writer), DeLillo might be able to describe the 1951 final in rich, vivid detail, but he cannot, and we cannot by extension, ever expect to feel like "a carrier of some solemn scrap of history," as Hodges felt after attending the Dempsey-Willard fight. Isn't this what tennis fans desire when straining to get a glimpse of Federer at Wimbledon? To see him in the flesh invites us to become physical carriers of a history that others can only access via film clips or written histories. You just had to be there, we tell others. Our physical presence at an event offers us the possibility of entrée into the sacredness of human history.

Of course, I'm speaking about the importance of *embodied experience*, and I contend that as modern living becomes increasingly focused on a kind of disembodied experience we yearn for embodiment more than ever. In fact, with the introduction of sound recordings, newsreels and television, it became possible for people to see or listen to historic events even if they were not present at the time. And thanks to the Internet we can go even further. We can watch Federer winning at Wimbledon or Jordan scoring in Salt Lake City, *any time we like*. And yet, ironically, all this access to recorded history, sporting or otherwise, hasn't dulled our interest in embodied experience; it has heightened it. Anyone can watch Michael Jordan's final shot on YouTube. Not everyone can say they were there. Few can say that they carry that scrap of history in their physical memory.

I was once boasting to an English friend that I had recently attended a U2 concert, and he casually informed me that he had seen them play live on twelve occasions. The first time was in a seedy pub in London with about one hundred people in the audience, and Bono and the Edge were snot-nosed Irish wannabe rock stars. Respect. Clearly, he carries a larger scrap of rock history than I do.

Carrying events in one's physical memory has been important as long ago as the birth of the church, where Justus and Matthias cast lots for Judas's vacant position among the ranks of the apostles. Peter had previously established the criterion for candidacy for such a position by announcing that an apostle must "have been with us the whole time the Lord Jesus was living among us, beginning from John's baptism to the time when Jesus was taken up from us. For one of these must become a witness with us of his resurrection" (Acts 1:21-22). Later, Paul would chafe under this restriction, arguing to the Corinthian church that he indeed had seen the risen Christ on the road to Damascus and therefore was qualified as a witness to the resurrection (1 Corinthians 9). I don't raise this to open a discussion about the biblical office of apostleship, but rather to point out that in the first-century church to have witnessed the resurrection carried greater weight than merely being able to say, "You ask me how I know he lives. He lives within my heart!"

This isn't much different to South Africans who refer to the "struggle credentials" of those who fought against apartheid last century. This "struggle legitimacy" afforded to long-time members and supporters of the African National Congress a higher level of social capital and a much stronger political, economic and moral mandate than other citizens. I once met in Cape Town a white South African doctor who had campaigned against apartheid during its darkest days, at great personal cost. He told me that he had been granted greater social legitimacy in ANC-run South Africa because of his struggle credentials, while other white citizens of his age were delegitimized for their lack of engagement in the struggle, even if they were ideologically opposed to apartheid. Physically bearing the burden of the struggle is revered more highly than simply believing in that struggle from the sidelines.

We know intuitively that embodied experience is of a higher order than vicarious experience. We hold dear the notion that *believing* in something is less important than also *doing* something about it. But this goes further than the usual faith-works dualism so often discussed in churches. It is about whether we know and carry the gospel in bodily forms, as well as in our so-called interior lives.

## CARRYING THE GOSPEL IN OUR BODIES

Of course, there are no living witnesses to the resurrection to be granted such "resurrection credentials" two thousand years after the fact. Nonetheless, we can affirm that our faith is not only a warm inner sense of conviction. John's testimony puts the lie to the notion that we know he lives only because he lives within our hearts: "We proclaim to you what we have seen and heard, so that you also may have fellowship with us. And our fellowship is with the Father and with his Son, Jesus Christ" (1 John 1:3). We know he lives, the Bible says, because the apostles tell us so. They were there, and it's in their confidence that we can embrace an incarnational faith in the absence of a physically present God.

An inner conviction or feeling is only worthwhile to the degree that it is embodied in action. As Johann Goethe said, "Whatever you think you can do or believe you can do, begin it. Action has magic, grace and power in it." There is indeed a kind of grace in action. We believe this when we baptize infants and new believers. Even those of us with the least sacramental views on baptism consider there to be something holy and blessed about the act of bearing the gospel in a physical form. In the tradition I belong to, we practice baptism by full immersion, believing there to be something important and powerful about reenacting the death and resurrection of Jesus by being buried under the water and resurrected with him to new life. The same can be said of the marriage ceremony. A couple can make the most sincere promises to each other in private, and they can be binding and meaningful. But in the Christian tradition we still expect that couple to appear before an assembly of their friends and family and enact those vows by giving and receiving rings.

However, the reenactment alone isn't what I'm promoting here. It's the public context of those reenactments. These sacramental rituals put skin on the incarnation in our day. When we can say, "I saw you get married (or baptized)," it carries weight—it's an independent verification, and it communicates accountability. "You had to be there" applies to both the agent (the person getting married or baptized) and the witness—not for both parties to be able to grasp the transcendence of the moment but for the transcendence to take place. It's the way we fulfill the idea that "you just had to be there."

In this way, sacramental acts like baptism, marriage and the Lord's Supper help us to become the physical carriers of that "solemn scrap of history," while knowing the gospel is far more than merely a scrap of history. But furthermore, all liturgical practice worthy of its intent should draw us physically into the story we hold dear. Whether we solemnly walk the Stations of the Cross or kneel to receive Holy Communion, whether we pray matins and vespers or take a daily "quiet time," we are enacting our faith, creating daily or weekly rhythms that draw us out of only living our faith in our "head" or "heart" and confirming our devotion in bodily forms. The bearers of the gospel today are invited into the action of God, to participate in the bringing of history to its true end. If we only live out our faith in our imagination and never express it in a rich rhythm of weekly practices, liturgies and activities, we are in danger of seeing the gospel only as offering a way for the redeemed soul to escape history.

For example, to say our faith helps us to have no fear of death means less than when we physically stare down death with serenity and resolve, our faith scaffolded by liturgy and practice. When John Wesley sailed to Georgia to commence missionary service among natives in North America, he found himself in a small ship in a fero-cious Atlantic storm and feared terribly for his life. In his journal he described the scene: "The sea broke over, split the mainsail in pieces, covered the ship, and poured in between the decks, as if the great deep had already swallowed us up. A terrible screaming began among the English."[3]

Being English himself, I've often wondered whether this was Wesley's oblique way of describing his own humiliating terror, the shame made all the more deep by the serenity of a band of Moravian missionaries from the Zinzendorf estate who continued to worship God calmly in the face of seemingly certain death. Astonished by their calm, Wesley approached them:

> I asked one of them afterwards, "Was you not afraid?" He answered, "I thank God, no." I asked, "But were not your women and children afraid?" He replied, mildly, "No; our women and children are not afraid to die." From them I went to their crying, trembling [English] neighbors, and pointed out to them the difference in the hour of trial, between him that feareth God, and him that feareth him not.[4]

This experience had a profound effect on the young Wesley. Coupled with his perceived lack of missionary success in Georgia, it caused him to question his resolve. If his faith made no difference in the face of a life-threatening storm, was it actually faith at all? Almost exactly two years to the day after his encounter with the Moravians he famously journaled his personal crisis:

> I went to America to convert the Indians; but oh! who shall convert me? . . . I have a fair summer religion. I can talk well; nay, and believe myself, while no danger is near; but let danger look me in the face, and my spirit is troubled. Nor can I say, "To die is gain!"[5]

Wesley is expressing the difference between a faith that one adopts cognitively and a faith that resides in one's very body. The Moravians he observed carried their faith in their nerve endings and their muscles, and it allowed them to calmly sing psalms in the midst of a tumult. It wasn't simply that they *knew* their faith more or better than John Wesley; their faith was an embodied experience, and in the face of danger it was expressed in liturgical fidelity. In this way, I believe, the Moravians were carrying the scrap of history in their bodies. They were carrying the gospel in their bodies, like a living record of life given, life healed, life hoped for. Storyteller Clarissa Pinkola Estes says,

> The body remembers, the bones remember, the joints re-member, even the little finger remembers. Memory is lodged ~~in pictures and feelings, in the cells themselves. Like a sponge~~ filled with water, anywhere the flesh is pressed, wrung, even touched lightly, a memory may flow out in a stream.[6]

The Moravians were true witnesses to the resurrection as embodied in their composed and tranquil worship. I believe their embodied faithfulness was not merely a state of mind but an action. They continued with the act of psalm singing despite the Atlantic Ocean rushing in upon them. Clearly affected by the dramatic power of liturgical devotion, John Wesley wrote that "there is no Liturgy in the world, either in ancient or modern language, which breathes more of a solid, scriptural, rational piety, than the Common Prayer of the Church of England."[7]

Later, when the American Methodists were separated from the Church of England, John Wesley himself provided a revised version of the Book of Common Prayer that included not only official liturgies but outlines for a daily office for all Methodists. And yet today we hear of Christians abandoning rituals and rhythms of worship or devotion, claiming that their relationship with Christ doesn't need imposed religious activity to sustain it. They end up engaging in their faith by cobbling together the input of televangelists or podcasts, blogs or social media, as though their faith is an entirely personal and private matter. They are as connected to their religious life as an ESPN viewer is to Roger Federer.

And now America's most successful churches are following suit. Research conducted by the University of Washington found that churches are now using stagecraft, sensory pageantry, charismatic leadership and an upbeat, unchallenging vision of Christianity to provide their congregants with a powerful emotional religious experience. James Wellman, associate professor of American religion at the University of Washington, and coauthors Katie E. Corcoran and Kate Stockly-Meyerdirk, studied 2008 data provided by the Leadership Network from twelve nationally representative American megachurches. Their paper was tellingly titled "'God is Like a Drug': Explaining Interaction Ritual Chains in American Megachurches." In it, they conclude that megachurch services feature a come-as-you-are atmosphere, rock music and a "multi-sensory mélange" of visuals and other elements to stimulate the senses, "creating membership feelings and symbols charged with emotional significance, and a heightened sense of spirituality."[8] While the report attempts to be even-handed, seeing the valuable and important contribution that megachurch worship makes to American Christianity, it also reveals the highly individualized and emotional culture it promulgates. Reporting on Wellman, Corcoran and Stockly-Meyerdirk's research, Peter Kelley says,

> Many participants used the word "contagious" to describe the feeling of a megachurch service where members arrive hungry for emotional experiences and leave energized. One church member said, "(T)he Holy Spirit goes through the crowd like a football team doing the wave. . . . Never seen it in any other

church." Wellman said, "That's what you see when you go into megachurches—you see smiling people; people who are dancing in the aisles. We see this experience of unalloyed joy over and over again in megachurches. That's why we say it's like a drug."[9]

I need to reiterate the point that I see nothing wrong with Christians connecting to God through their emotions. We are emotional and imaginative beings, and worshiping God emotionally and imaginatively is a perfectly legitimate thing to do. Though, if this is the *only* way—or even the primary way—in which we experience God and express our faith, we are on very thin ice. We are being swept up into an excarnate culture that seems to only experience things emotionally or imaginatively. As noted earlier, Charles Taylor discusses this as "the transfer of our religious life out of bodily forms of ritual, worship, practice, so that it comes more and more to reside 'in the head.'"[10] Disembodied faith, a form of religious belief that tickles the fancy and titillates the imagination but never seeps into our flesh, into action, service and liturgy, can legitimately be called excarnate faith. It has no struggle credentials. In its Christian form it's like treating Jesus as an online boyfriend or watching him do his thing on YouTube.

## THE INCARNATION AS THE ORDER OF THINGS

The New Living Translation of Colossians 2:9 reads, "For in Christ lives all the fullness of God *in a human body*." C. S. Lewis once remarked that, "The central miracle asserted by Christians is the Incarnation. They say that God became Man. Every other miracle prepares for this, or exhibits this, or results from this."[11] The enfleshing of God in the person of Jesus stands at the center of our faith. All that Israel hoped for was realized in him. The resurrection proceeds from it, as does the birth of the church and the gift of the

Holy Spirit. Therefore, any drift toward excarnate forms of faith denies in some measure the central nature of our faith. Watching Charles Stanley on television or listening to podcasts of John Piper's sermons might be helpful in all sorts of ways, but it isn't the same as physically gathering with brothers and sisters around the Bible and embracing the embodied task of being a hermeneutic community—that is, a community that interprets the text collectively. Embodiment is costly in a way that excarnate forms of religious faith are not. As the people of the incarnate One, we must allow that "central miracle" to shape our lives, recognizing that the incarnation came at great personal cost to God, that it required of him a descent into brokenness and a reascent to glory, and that it must be embodied in a similarly costly fashion in our churches today.

Jesus himself not only embodied this pattern, he explicitly taught it. In John 12:24 he says, "Very truly I tell you, unless a kernel of wheat falls to the ground and dies, it remains only a single seed. But if it dies, it produces many seeds." I love C. S. Lewis's beautiful take on this: "Certainly no seed ever fell from so fair a tree into so dark and cold a soil." Jesus' word here is usually taken to refer to his impending crucifixion, but I'm with Lewis in believing it is more helpfully understood as a reference to the whole story of the incarnation. From start to finish, God descends to reascend. Like a husk of wheat or the fruit of the vine, it must belittle itself into something hard, small and deathlike, it must fall into the ground: therein the new life reascends. C. S. Lewis sees the incarnation as the pattern of the embodied life to which we've all been called:

> So it is also in our moral and emotional life. The first innocent and spontaneous desires have to submit to the deathlike process of control or total denial: but from that there is a reascent to fully formed character in which the strength of the original material all operates but in a new way. Death and

Rebirth—go down to go up—it is a key principle. Through
this bottleneck, this belittlement, the highroad nearly always
lies. The doctrine of the Incarnation, if accepted, puts this
principle even more emphatically at the center.[12]

Submitting oneself to this bottleneck is an embodied exercise. One
cannot simply speak of this death as metaphysical when Jesus
himself doesn't. It requires real action. For example, it's worth
noting that the Bible never speaks about having humble feelings.
In discussing humility Scripture never refers to one's attitude or
feelings about oneself. Indeed, when the humility of Jesus is discussed in the Bible, there is no mention of him having a low view
of himself. Rather, humility in his life and the rest of the New
Testament is a *doing word*—it refers to the action of a strong person
deliberately stepping down to serve others. And in the most sus-
tained discussion of Jesus' humility, Philippians 2:5-11, we see that
Jesus chose the belittling course, by choosing to be a servant of all,
thus showing the path of glory (the "road up," in Lewis' parlance)
is the path of giving up. Of course, Paul begins this meditation on
Jesus' humility by insisting that his followers "have the same
mindset as Christ Jesus" (Philippians 2:5), therein making the assumption that the church would embrace their vocation to physically embody humility, to submit to the lowering of ourselves in
the service of others, believing that in so doing the road up could
be reached.

I recall being in the audience at the U2 concert I mentioned a
little earlier when front man Bono started in on a sermon about
world poverty, clicking his fingers and telling us that every second
somewhere around the world a child was dying of preventable
causes. His call to the audience to rally together to make poverty
history was met with a rousing chorus of cheers from the thousands
in attendance. "Together we can do it!" he shouted triumphantly.

The audience went wild. Later that night, as we filed out of the stadium, I noticed people wending their way around the homeless panhandlers who had positioned themselves outside the gates, refusing to make eye contact with them, refusing their requests for assistance. Their response to the rally call to end poverty earlier in the night was merely the expression of collective feelings. It had no demonstration in action or service or humility. It was an excarnate response to poverty. It was lived "in the head" but not enacted in our bodies. Everyone wanted to take the "road up" to a poverty-free world, but no one was willing to get there via the road down, into the gutter, among the poor themselves. But the incarnation teaches us that the way up is via the downward road.

# 6

## Learning Embodiment
## from the Master

*Jesus's resurrection is the beginning of God's new project
not to snatch people away from earth to heaven but
to colonize earth with the life of heaven.*

N. T. WRIGHT

I f you've watched Joe Wright's film *The Soloist* you will have seen this
idea played out quite powerfully. It's based on a true story in
which Robert Downey Jr. plays Steve Lopez, a journalist with the
*LA Times*, who encounters a schizophrenic homeless man, Nathaniel Ayers (Jamie Foxx), exquisitely playing a battered violin
on the streets of Los Angeles. After some investigation, Lopez discovers that Ayers was once a child prodigy, until he began dis-
playing symptoms of schizophrenia while studying at Juilliard.
Unable to deal with the voices in his head, Ayers dropped out and
ended up on the streets. Lopez thinks the story is too good not to
tell, so he makes it the subject for his newspaper column. Little
does he know that he's begun the journey downward.

One of his readers is so touched, she sends Lopez a cello for

Ayers. This forces Lopez to search out Ayers again and deliver the instrument to him, and in so doing he descends a little further downward. Lopez seems to think that after giving Ayers the cello his connection with Ayers will end. However, Ayers's mental state means that he is no position to take care of the valuable instrument. Lopez is so concerned for the well-being of the generous gift he talks him into leaving it at a local homeless shelter. Lopez's journey downward continues. Wanting to free himself from any further obligation to Ayers, but feeling increasing responsible for him, Lopez attempts to provide him with medical care and housing, and even persuades a friend to try to rehabilitate Ayers through music lessons. But in his unstable state, Ayers eventually threatens Lopez and attacks his new cello teacher. The further down Lopez goes with Ayers the further he feels drawn into his life, even though he is desperately trying to extricate himself from it.

Lopez voices his frustration at Ayers's regular relapses and his seeming lack of gratitude for all he has done for him, to his ex-wife and editor, Mary (Catherine Keener), who in a moment of clarity points out that he has to stop trying to "fix" Nathaniel and start just being his friend. This scene marks the point at which Lopez hits the bottom of his downward journey. He has been belittled and bowed, and now realizes his mistake in trying to perform some miraculous therapeutic act in Ayers's life and get out as quick as he can. Ayers's presence in his life isn't a simple project to be completed; it is an opportunity to true friendship—messy, frustrating, joyful and unending. By coming to this moment of enlightenment he has followed the road down until it has turned upward. The film ends with Lopez, in voiceover, saying:

> There are people who tell me I've helped him. Mental health experts who say that the simple act of being someone's friend can change his brain chemistry, improve his functioning in

the world. I can't speak for Mr. Ayers in that regard. Maybe our friendship has helped him, but maybe not. I can, however, speak for myself. I can tell you that by witnessing Mr. Ayers's courage, his humility, his faith in the power of his art, I've learned the dignity of being loyal to something you believe in. Of holding onto it, above all else. Of believing, without question, that it will carry you home.

Earlier, I quoted C. S. Lewis saying, "Through this bottleneck, this belittlement, the highroad nearly always lies." It is the way of Jesus, and even filmmakers like Joe Wright have intuited its wonderful truth. And yet, while Steve Lopez is drawn reluctantly into the world of Nathanael Ayers, Jesus wades chest deep into the wretchedness of our world with his eyes wide open, fully cognizant of all that he is doing. The incarnation is not God's attempt to fix humankind by getting in and out as quickly as he can. It was God's plan for fashioning friendship between himself and us. It is like all true friendship—messy, frustrating, joyful and unending.

This is where we can as legitimately experience the presence and empowerment of God as is experienced in an emotional megachurch worship gathering. Indeed, I think when we can find God in the wretchedness of this world we are connecting to a more authentic and sustaining faith than one that is only experienced via the multisensory mélange of elements designed to stimulate our senses in church services.

## JESUS AS THE EMBODIED NEW ISRAEL

When we look at the life of Jesus we discover that he embraced embodiment not only to pattern the order of things to us, but the incarnation reveals that Jesus physically embraces his vocation to embody the very history of Israel even as he is lifting the curse Israel had been burdened with.

This is seen in the holy family's flight to Egypt, but more pointedly in their return to Israel from exile. As Mathew's Gospel explains, "And so was fulfilled what the Lord had said through the prophet: 'Out of Egypt I called my son'" (Matthew 2:15). Matthew clearly has in mind the reference in Hosea 11:1: "When Israel was a child, I loved him, and out of Egypt I called my son." In this way Jesus' return to his homeland was a kind of embodied replay of Israel's flight from Egypt.

Furthermore, Jesus commences his public ministry by submitting to baptism at the hands of his cousin John, symbolizing Israel's escape through the Red Sea, immediately after which he embodies Israel's wilderness experience (Matthew 4:1-11). Three times, Matthew tells us, the tempter came to Jesus, inviting him to do as Israel had done during their time in the wilderness and abandon their fidelity to Yahweh. On all three occasions Jesus resists temptation by quoting Scripture, but it's important to note what Scriptures he utilizes to repel the tempter: "Man does not live on bread alone . . ." (Deuteronomy 8:3); "Do not put the LORD your God to the test" (Deuteronomy 6:16); and "Worship the Lord your God, and serve him only" (Deuteronomy 6:12-13). All three texts are quotations attributed to Moses during Israel's wandering in the desert. In effect, Jesus is embodying the history of Israel, but *doing it right this time!*

After forty days in the desert, Jesus provocatively appoints twelve apostles (Mark 3:13-19) and then explicitly invites them to see themselves as a correlation to the twelve tribes of Israel: "Truly I tell you, at the renewal of all things, when the Son of Man sits on his glorious throne, you who have followed me will also sit on twelve thrones, judging the twelve tribes of Israel" (Matthew 19:28). As Graham Stanton says,

> The importance of the call of the twelve can scarcely be exaggerated. In this prophetic action Jesus is calling for the re-

newal of Israel. He is also expressing the conviction that God
is now beginning to establish his people anew—and will bring
this promise to fulfillment.[1]

More than that, he is establishing his people anew by embodying
their history, righting their wrongs, satisfying their covenant with
Yahweh and undoing the curse that had been placed on them. This
can't be understated. Many Jews in Jesus' time saw themselves as
living under the curses they were warned about long before in such
passages as Deuteronomy 28, the description of the blessings and
curses that would be visited upon Israel if they did or didn't keep
their covenant with God. The curses included destruction by their
enemies and plagues of fevers, boils and blindness (see Deuteronomy 28:15-28). By the time of Jesus, after their defeats at the
hands of the Assyrians (eighth century B.C.), the Babylonians (sixth
century B.C.), the Greeks (fourth and third centuries B.C.) and most
recently the Romans (first century B.C.), Jewish people were convinced they were being punished for their infidelity. Furthermore,
their country was beset by the very diseases named in Deuteronomy
28. Their only hope was derived from the various Old Testament
prophesies about a coming Day of Lord where the anointed servant
of God would undo the effects of the curse.

Seen in this light, the picture of the incarnate One wading into
a sea of sickness and disease, curing the blind and the lame and
freeing the demon-possessed reveals the degree to which Jesus embodied Israel's story and called them into the renewal and hope only
he could offer. He is physically lifting the curse, undoing the effects
of generations of fear and faithlessness within Israel.

Clearly, the alternative to excarnate faith is embracing an incarnational expression of following Jesus. In this respect I take *incarnational* to mean three things: (1) being patterned on the incarnation,
(2) being enabled by the continuing power of the incarnation,

and (3) joining the ongoing incarnational mission of God.[2] I take to heart that Jesus is the one-and-only incarnation. He is not the first of multiple incarnations. Many people may live lives of sacrificial service and devotion to God, and some may even die in such service and devotion, but Jesus alone is God incarnate. I believe that apart from this unique divine act, Jesus' work on our behalf would have no saving value. While it is Jesus' unique vocation to physically lift the curse on Israel, something no human—Jewish or otherwise—can achieve, his life and teaching and the gift of his Spirit nonetheless commission us into his service. So when I call us to embrace an incarnational lifestyle, I am not suggesting we are all Christs, far from it! I am asking us to be open to being filled by the Spirit of the incarnate One, to pattern our lives on his example and to commit ourselves to participate in God's work of bringing history to its true end. I can't explain this more eloquently than Karl Barth, who said,

> Faith is not concerned with a special realm, that of religion, say, but with real life in its totality, the outward as well as the inward questions, that which is bodily as well as that which is spiritual, the brightness as well as the gloom in our life. Faith is concerned with our being permitted to rely on God as regards ourselves and also as regards what moves us on behalf of others, of the whole of humanity; it is concerned with the whole of living and the whole of dying. The freedom to have this trust (understood in this comprehensive way) is faith.[3]

## ELBOW LEARNING

The embrace of a missional-incarnational impulse should be seen primarily as a response to the grace of Jesus and a desire to honor and worship the Trinity, the sent-and-sending God. Having fulfilled God's covenant with Israel, and having lifted the curse on human-

kind, Jesus co-opts his followers into the exciting task of bringing
history to its true end. Our challenge is to learn ways to bodily
embrace this task, to physically wade into the brokenness of humankind and alert people to the universal reign of God through
Christ. The term we use for this is *discipleship*, and as we will see
in chapter seven, the journey of a disciple can never be reduced
merely to an intellectual exercise. True disciples bear the bodily
weight of truth, carrying the gospel in their lifestyles and the
rhythms of their collective life. If God reveals himself most sub-
limely in the incarnation, then it follows that the journey of discipleship must be learned incarnationally. No mere formulas or
simple steps can suffice. In his book *Personal Knowledge*, philosopher Michael Polanyi wrote, "practical wisdom is more truly embodied in action than expressed in rules of action."[4]

It has been noted in various quarters that the half-illiterate Italian
violin maker Antonio Stradivari never recorded the exact plans or
dimensions for how to make one of his famous instruments. This
might have been a commercial decision (during the earliest years
of the 1700s, Stradivari's violins were in high demand and open to
being copied by other luthiers). But it might also have been because,
well, Stradivari didn't know exactly how to record their dimensions,
their weight and their balance. He knew how to create a violin with
his hands and his fingers, but maybe not in figures kept in the head
or recorded in notebooks.

Today, those violins, named after the Latinized form of his name
Stradivarius, are considered priceless. It is believed there are only
around five hundred of them still in existence, some of which have
been submitted to the most intense scientific examination in an
attempt to reproduce their extraordinary sound quality. But no one
has been able to replicate Stradivari's craftsmanship.

They've worked out that he used spruce for the top, and willow
for the internal blocks and linings, and maple for the back, ribs and

neck. They've figured out that he also treated the wood with several types of minerals, including potassium borate, sodium and potassium silicate, as well as a handmade varnish that appears to have been composed of gum arabic, honey and egg white. But they still can't replicate a Stradivarius.

The genius craftsman never once recorded his technique for posterity. Instead, he passed on his knowledge to a number of his apprentices via what Polanyi calls elbow learning. This is the process where a protégé is trained in a new art or skill by sitting at the elbow of a master, learning their craft through doing it, copying it, not simply by reading about it. The apprentices of the great Stradivari didn't learn their craft from books or manuals, but by sitting at his elbow and feeling the wood as he felt it, to assess its length, its balance, its timbre, right in their fingertips. All the learning happened at his elbow, and all the knowledge was contained in his fingers.

Michael Polanyi insists that we recover our capacity to learn like Stradivari's protégés, by feeling the weight of a piece of wood, not by reading the prescribed measurements in a manual. He says,

> To learn by example is to submit to authority. You follow your master because you trust his manner of doing things even when you cannot analyze and account in detail for its effectiveness. By watching the master and emulating his efforts in the presence of his example, the apprentice unconsciously picks up the rules of the art, including those which are not explicitly known to the master himself. These hidden rules can be assimilated only by a person who surrenders himself to that extent uncritically to the imitation of the master.[5]

This is the way of the incarnational Christian. To draw near to the Master we must learn discipleship in our fingertips, not just in our "heads." Instead of churning out books, manuals, DVDs, podcasts, websites, tweets, status updates, Jesus took a band of protégés to his elbow and humbly but relentlessly passed on the "hidden rules" of service. Like Jesus, incarnational leaders model it, live it, breathe it and invite others to copy them. In this vein, we might recall the words of St. Paul writing to the Corinthians, "Follow my example, as I follow the example of Christ" (1 Corinthians 11:1). Now that's elbow learning.

In *Unleader*, Lance Ford says,

> We need real, breathing, walking around, hands and feet, human examples; followers that are following Jesus. This is essential and without substitute. The example of Jesus, alive in the framework of living flesh and blood, gives the greatest reference for potential followers to follow. Jesus demonstrates that the gospel message is something that can tangibly be lived.[6]

Compare this to the story of the young Albert Einstein traveling through Europe on a lecture tour of the great universities. He had employed one of his doctoral students to accompany him as his general assistant and driver. At each school Einstein delivered exactly the same lecture on the application of his general theory of relativity to model the structure of the universe as a whole. This became increasingly monotonous for both the professor and his student driver, and so to alleviate the boredom Einstein and his protégé decided to mix things up a bit at the next lecture by switching places. Einstein was not yet internationally famous, so no one would know if his student appeared on the platform instead of him. The student had heard the presentation scores of times so he could deliver it as faultlessly as his teacher.

At the next university the student passed himself off to their hosts as Einstein, and the great scientist was introduced as his student and driver. No one was any the wiser. Indeed, no one knew anything was amiss during the lecture, which the student delivered flawlessly while Einstein sat smirking in the front row. However, at the end of the presentation, the host professor did something that no other host had done during the lecture tour. He invited the audience to ask questions.

The blood drained from the fake Einstein's face as a physics professor in the audience asked a particularly difficult question about statistical mechanics and quantum theory, particle theory and the motion of molecules. Einstein himself blanched, knowing the game was up. Then the student composed himself and continued the ruse: "That question is so simple it insults my intelligence. And to prove it I'm going to ask my chauffeur to answer it."

Stradivari's protégés knew how to make a violin because they had sat at their master's elbow; they had imbibed all that he knew about his craft; they had measured every aspect of the instrument with their own hands after watching him measure it with his. Einstein's student knew how to recite a lecture without knowing all there was to know about the theory of relativity.

I fear we are living through a time where, once again, knowledge has been reduced to simple steps or memorable formulas, where authors are purveying models they claim anyone can quickly adopt, where conference speakers are dishing up five of their seven steps for effective leadership and then encouraging audiences to buy their latest book for the last two steps. But too many so-called leaders only know one lecture's worth of material. They need their fingertips to be dried out by handling spruce and for their nostrils to be filled with willow sawdust. They need to sit for hours on end at their master's workbench, to humble themselves enough to learn, to suffer, to sacrifice, to be shaped into the likeness of the master craftsman.

### The Big Fisherman

This kind of elbow learning is beautifully illustrated by Jesus' calling of Peter by the Sea of Galilee (Luke 5). From the bow of a fishing boat Jesus taught a crowd assembled on the shore. Afterward, Jesus asks Peter, the owner of the boat, to put out into deep water and let out the nets for a catch. You can hear the frustration and weariness in Peter's voice when he replies, "Master, we've worked hard all night and haven't caught anything. But because you say so, I will let down the nets" (v. 5). The resulting catch was so enormous that Peter's boat nearly sank, leading to his terrified response to Jesus, "Go away from me, Lord; I am a sinful man!" (v. 7). Immediately after this episode Jesus calls Peter as his disciple and promises that from that time forth he will be fishing for people, not fish. I find interesting that in the calling of the first disciples we see nature, humans and God all woven together in ways that affirm their essential connectedness. Following Jesus isn't merely the intellectual affirmation of his teaching. It is our whole world coming under his reign.

Note the way Jesus reaches out to Peter by asking for his help, not by offering it. He deliberately places himself in a position where he genuinely needs the help of the one he invites into discipleship. And it is an authentic request, not a contrived one. Jesus needs Peter's boat and fishing skills, and so Peter's worth is thereby affirmed on his own terms. Jesus' ministry becomes a partnership with Peter. Every master needs an apprentice. It's not a one-way process. Of course, the master is passing on valuable skills, but the partnership is essential and an important intimacy develops. We rightly say that God has no need of us, that he is whole and complete in and of himself. But the beauty and scandal of the gospel is that God in Christ takes on flesh and asks for our help, and in doing so he radically transforms us into the incarnational followers he desires. As Kenneth Bailey describes this episode:

> In this story matter/mammon/money are woven together with
> the things of the spirit. Peter faces a man who wins the "fishing

lottery" but doesn't want it. Stunned, Peter realizes the inadequacy of his own values and priorities. The impact on him, by the gentle man who radically re-absolutizes mammon, is enormous. Taking his former skills with him, he moves forward into a new venture of faith.[7]

Jesus takes a fisherman and transforms him into the "big fisherman." When we find ourselves at Jesus' elbow, we will find ourselves in a unique and wonderful intimacy with him, not one where he destroys us and totally remakes us from nothing, but an apprenticeship where he takes what we are and reshapes us into something bigger for his glory and service.

# 7

# Desire, Idolatry and Discipleship

*Christianity got over the difficulty of combining*
*furious opposites by keeping them both,*
*and keeping them both furious.*

G. K. CHESTERTON

⑤

**I have argued that we are adopting** an increasingly excarnate approach to faith, allowing our engagement with God to reside almost entirely in our imaginations. I would also suggest that such a drift toward excarnation is made possible by similarly disembodied approaches to doing theology. By developing a theology of persons that focuses chiefly, or even solely, on human as primarily thinking beings and not as fully embodied creatures leads to an insufficient anthropology that owes more to modernity and the Enlightenment than it does to the holistic, biblical vision of human persons. Excarnation—the steady disembodiment of spiritual life, so that it is less and less carried in deeply meaningful bodily forms and lies more and more in the head—demonstrates that insufficient theological reflection on the nature of humanness doesn't help.

However, an interesting new anthropology, drawing in some cases on classic Christian theology, is coming to our rescue. A new biblical understanding of human persons is emerging, and it gives us hope that we can resist the excarnate impulses in society today. I want to explore three broad areas of theological reflection on anthropology that together can contribute to this more holistic understanding. First, C. S. Lewis's understanding that all human longing is a quest for God helps to validate physical impulses while infusing them with redemptive possibilities. Second, both James K. A. Smith's appropriation of the Augustinian idea of rightly ordered loves and Tim Keller's recent work on idolatry invite us to live as disciples in fully enfleshed ways. Third, I will undergird these ideas by asking questions about a Christian theology of persons, one that doesn't allow us to retreat into the old body-soul dualism, but which frames self-understanding in more biblically holistic ways.

## THE SCENT OF A FLOWER WE HAVE NOT FOUND

In a time when it was standard practice for preachers to speak about the "inner man" as distinct from a person's outward actions and choices, C. S. Lewis argued for a far greater integration in our understanding of human yearning and choice. In other words, the distinction between *being* and *doing*, so common these days, is roundly rejected by Lewis. Let's begin our brief look at Lewis's anthropology by exploring his fascination with *Sehnsucht*. Often translated as "life longing," the German word *Sehnsucht* is difficult to translate adequately but is used to describe a deep emotional state in which a person reflects on unfinished or imperfect facets of life and yearns for more, for ideal alternative experiences. *Sehnsucht* often feels like the longing for a far-off country, a place we've never visited but which strangely feels like "home." It is a type of nostalgia, in the original sense of that word. *Sehnsucht* took on a particular significance in Lewis's work, who described it as the "inconsolable longing" in the human heart for "we know not what." In

the preface to *The Pilgrim's Regress* he touchingly described those
things that touched off a feeling of *Sehnsucht* in him:

> That unnameable something, desire for which pierces us like
> a rapier at the smell of bonfire, the sound of wild ducks flying
> overhead, the title of *The Well at the World's End*, the opening
> lines of *Kubla Khan*, the morning cobwebs in late summer, or
> the noise of falling waves.[1]

For Lewis, paying attention to *Sehnsucht*, our deepest longings, was
a clue to the true nature of humankind. This is distinct from an
excarnate-style theology that repudiates all human longing as sinful
and insists on a bifurcated human being that is either good or bad.
Like the white angel and the red devil that sits on the shoulders of
cartoon characters when faced with a moral choice, dualistic theology separates humankind into sin and grace, bad and good, black
and white, flesh and soul. Lewis was far more sophisticated than
that. He dared to suggest that *all* human longing was good in that
it propels the person toward God. However, it became sinful when
the person stopped short of pursuing this longing to its ultimate
end and settled for something less. Lewis explored this idea in his
famous sermon "The Weight of Glory," in which he sought to separate the means of measuring God's grace from grace itself. His
point is that we often sense something sublime and truthful and
beautiful in all manner of things—literature, art, music, food,
falling in love—but we mistakenly imagine the thing itself is
truthful or beautiful, but in fact it is merely a conduit for truth or
beauty to be conveyed to us from God. As an example, he refers to
the way we encounter beauty in great literature and beautiful music:

> The books or the music in which we thought the beauty was
> located will betray us if we trust to them; it was not in them,
> it only came through them, and what came through them was

longing. These things—the beauty, the memory of our own past—are good images of what we really desire; but if they are mistaken for the thing itself they turn into dumb idols, breaking the hearts of their worshippers.[2]

In a second example, he refers to the pleasure experienced in human friendship as opening us to the presence of and longing for God:

> When four or five of us after a hard day's walking have come to our inn; when our slippers are on, our feet spread out towards the blaze, and our drinks at our elbows; when the whole world, *and something beyond the world*, opens itself to our minds as we talk. Life—natural life—has no better gift to give.[3]

Note Lewis's deft argument that what we experience when we feel drawn to these potential idols is longing itself, and we do well to pay attention to such longing, for ultimately it can lead us to the true and ultimate object of all human longing—God. When we find ourselves yearning for success or romance or beauty, we are indeed yearning for God. Lewis explains, "For they are not the thing itself; they are only the scent of a flower we have not found, the echo of a tune we have not heard, news from a country we have never yet visited."[4]

Or put another way, as G. K. Chesterton is noted for having said, "Every man who knocks on the door of a brothel is looking for God." Like news from a far-off land, like the whiff of an unseen flower, like echoes of an unheard tune, the things in this world that turn our heads lead us ultimately to God if we follow those yearnings to their ultimate end. Human longing itself isn't sinful, to be ignored, denied or rejected. Quite the opposite, it provides clues to the object of our true quest. Put simply, our longings for a successful career or a happy family or for beauty, pleasure or adventure are godly yearnings, but when we make these pursuits ends in themselves, no matter how noble they might be, they become idolatrous. The ultimate expression of sin is when we cease exploring the source of human yearning and therefore do not discover it is a hunger for God. Lewis describes it this way: "Here, then, is the desire, still wandering and uncertain of its object and still largely unable to see that object in the direction where it really lies."[5] Our desire is blind, stumbling in darkness, smelling a fragrance it cannot identify, searching for the source of the satisfaction of all human yearning. As Lewis once claimed, "If I find in myself a desire which no experience in this world can satisfy, the most probable explanation is that I was made for another world."[6]

This approach leads us to abandon the dualism of spiritual and physical pursuits, as though church going is a spiritual exercise while gardening or mathematics are entirely profane ventures. Instead, all human longing is affirmed as a quest for God, and all human activity condoned by Scripture is potentially godly when pursued as an expression of worship of the sovereign God.

## RIGHTLY ORDERED LOVES

A similar point is made by James K. A. Smith in his book *Desiring the Kingdom: Worship, Worldview, and Cultural Formation*, where he takes his readers to task for an inadequate biblical anthropology. Building more on Augustine than Lewis, he nonetheless affirms Lewis's belief in the importance of longing in a theology of human persons. Smith though prefers the term *desire*. His Augustinian approach to understanding humanness forms the second of the three broad areas I want to discuss.

Smith's central thesis is that attempting to become fully human purely by the transfer of information is not formative enough, no matter how good that information may be or how well it is presented. The overly cognitive model he is critiquing assumes that if we teach people the Bible effectively enough, we will change and become more the people God intended us to be. We hear this kind of rationale being presented by some in the so-called neo-Calvinist movement, which emphasizes Reformed teaching over all other expressions of Christian service. For Smith, however, the leverage point for meaningful discipleship isn't an increased intellectual appreciation of a biblical worldview but a shift in our core desires. In other words, the starting point for Smith's model is desire rather than worldview:

> Before we articulate a worldview, we worship. . . . That's the kind of animals we are, first and foremost: loving, desiring, affective, liturgical animals who, for the most part, don't inhabit the world as thinkers or cognitive machines. . . . [G]iven the sorts of animals we are, we pray *before* we believe, we worship before we know—or rather, we worship *in order* to know.[7]

Smith goes on to call for an Augustinian renewal of our understanding of the human person, primarily as "embodied agents of desire or love."[8] Our desires are primarily expressed by our actions. Christian formation, then, is not chiefly concerned with subduing our despicable bodies and replenishing our souls or imaginations. At its heart the growth of the Christian person is a journey toward, as Augustine would say, rightly ordered loves, which leads to right living. This journey is, unfortunately, a road less traveled than that laid out for us by the dualistic, Neo-Platonic worldview that characterizes our excarnate age. Augustine himself had some difficulty abandoning the lingering Neo-Platonism of his Manichaean background, but Smith's retake reminds us that several features of Augustine's work are very helpful in a time of excarnation such as ours.

First, his insistence that we look at our actions or habits and their motivating desires as the starting point in the quest for truth is epistemologically and existentially evocative, and forms a helpful alternative to the carnivalesque Western culture that places the ex-

ternal, the trivial and the material foremost in our minds. As Charles
Taylor said, "Augustine was the first to make the first-person stand-
point fundamental to our search for truth."[9] This isn't to affirm
some new-age quest for the "truth within" but simply acknowledges that we must take human longing into account when
searching for ultimate truth. It also implies that human longing is
never simply some interior thing. We experience longing physically,
and we demonstrate it palpably and in action.

Following on from that, Augustine's focus on the search for happiness as our existential prime mover not only still rings true but
has been proven time and again to be accurate. Augustine's analysis
shakes up our superficial understandings of happiness and offers a
challenging alternative, namely, that ultimate happiness is not to be
found in the elusive character of the American dream, but is rather
transcendent in origin and nature. It's this point that James K. A.
Smith focuses on so richly in *Desiring the Kingdom*, and in doing so
he pursues Augustine's concept of disordered love, in which the
soul seeks satisfaction (or happiness) in things that are metaphysi-
cally incapable of providing it. For Augustine the concept of disordered love is the repeated, desperate attempt to achieve happiness
by satisfying all desires in objects that ultimately never satisfy. The
Bible calls this *idolatry*. Paul would call it *unrighteousness*. Today's
psychotherapist would probably label it *addiction* or *dysfunction*.
For Lewis, this is pulling up short of pursuing longing to its ultimate end. In pointing this out, Augustine has put his finger on the
pulse of our times.

But more than diagnosis, Augustine offers us the cure for our
disordered loves by insisting that God is the key to happiness, the
summum bonum, the fulfillment of the abyss in the human heart.
Put simply, we engage the world as lovers, and what we love defines
us. To rightly order our loves we must see God as our priority and
properly order our love for other things accordingly. While God

should be this ultimate love, sin has distorted our affections and pointed them toward things that are not God. Much of the time these things are not inherently bad. Rather, they are usually good things, but to hold anything other than God as ultimate in our lives is idolatry.

Think of human desires being ranked along a vertical grid, with God ranked most highly and sinful things ranked least. There is usually a straightforward distinction drawn between desiring God on the one hand and desiring violence or vengeance or greed or gluttony on the other. Ranking God above these things is obviously the right thing to do. Even though we still find ourselves giving into vengeance or lust or greed at times, it's not that we weren't aware that they are wrong. The more subtle distinction for us, and the one that trips us up more often, is the ranking of noble pursuits—family, beauty, art, music, fellowship and so forth—under God (see fig.7.1).

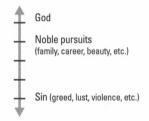

**Figure 7.1. Ranking of human desires**

Unpacking this, James K. A. Smith rightly notes that the issue of love is essentially an issue of worship: "our ultimate love is what we worship."[10] That is to say, we *act* upon our loves. Agreeing with Augustine that our affections have been diverted toward lesser things, he goes on to engage with love's end or *telos*. What we love is ultimately rooted in some kind of picture of human flourishing. Whatever supreme picture of human flourishing we hold will then govern the way we act, think, decide and love. It is here that Smith argues persuasively for his anthropology of the human person primarily as lover:

> Rather than being pushed by beliefs, we are pulled by a *telos* that we desire. It's not so much that we're intellectually convinced and then we muster the willpower to pursue what we ought; rather, at a precognitive level, we are attracted to a vision of the good life that has been painted for us in stories and myths, images and icons.[11]

That's purely Augustinian. We form a picture of what true human happiness looks like and then we unconsciously pursue that picture. It's less about our worldview than it is about our core or innate desires or hungers. But more than that, our habits also help to shape this picture, and, as Smith shows, this must be taken into account when thinking through the nature and shape of Christian formation. In this way, cultural practices and institutions become kinds of liturgies and create what Smith calls "cultural pedagogies." For example, often when people are bored or restless they turn on the television, check social media or go to the shopping mall. These actions, Smith asserts, are cultural habits that then in turn reassert certain values or disordered loves. Something as seemingly mundane as shopping at the mall becomes a powerful liturgical event that has a dramatic effect on our vision of human flourishing. It satisfies our boredom at one level, but it also reinforces consumerism, materialism and greed at another. Our desire for happiness unconsciously shapes what we pursue in life, and those pursuits return the favor by increasingly shaping our desires. Smith outlines several "secular liturgies," such as shopping and university education, showing their formative nature and the subtle ways they direct our desires.

Fundamentally, the concern was to emphasize that Christianity is not only (or even primarily) a set of cognitive, heading

> beliefs; Christianity is not fundamentally a worldview. . . .
> Rather, we sought to show that what Christians think and
> believe (and they do think and believe, and that's a good
> thing!) grows out of *what Christians do*.[12]

Here Smith very helpfully affirms the holistic view of human
persons that the biblical writers themselves would have held. If we
rightly order our desires, the success of our quest for happiness is
assured, but what we do matters, not just what we think. And every
trip to the shopping mall, every television commercial, every engagement at work invites us to do other than we were called to do.
The struggle for Christians and church leaders is to explore what
practices, liturgies or habits need to be cultivated in our lives to
countermand the domination of ungodly cultural pedagogies. More
on this later.

In *The Shaping of Things to Come* I explored the need to shift our
emphasis from orthodoxy to orthopraxy, questioning the usual
belief that getting our creeds right necessarily leads to right living.[13]
With my coauthor, Alan Hirsch, I suggested that missional *action*
draws the believer into right living, which in turn shapes right
thinking. James K. A. Smith prefers to root orthopraxy in the nature
and practices of Christian *worship*. I want to say more about this
later, but for now I will agree with him that we can't simply teach
Christians right theology and assume it alone will shape godly disciples. In fact, an emphasis on teaching alone plays into the hands
of our worst and most excarnate impulses. We must go deeper. If
human beings are primarily creatures of desire, the goal of a
Christian education must seek to influence these desires, helping
others to gain a biblical picture of human flourishing, rightly or-
dering all loves around the universal reign of God.

# 8

# We Are Spirited Bodies

*Humans are amphibians—half spirit and half animal.*
*. . . As spirits they belong to the eternal world, but as animals*
*they inhabit time. This means that while their spirit can be directed*
*to an eternal object, their bodies, passions, and imaginations are*
*in continual change, for to be in time, means to change.*

C. S. LEWIS

referred earlier to John Wesley's encounter with the worshiping Moravians on board a storm-tossed ship. Their panic-free worship was an expression of rightly ordered loves. But their loves were rightly ordered by their commitment to liturgy and an habitual life. This is stunningly portrayed in French director Xavier Beauvois' film *Of Gods and Men*. Based on the true story of the kidnapping and murder of Cistercian monks in Algeria by Muslim fundamentalists in 1996, it takes us into the claustrophobic world of a group of Christian men facing imminent martyrdom. As the film opens we see the monks have developed a happy relationship with the local Muslim villagers, based partly on the free outpatient clinic they provide. They have a quiet, supportive respect for each other's traditions. But a sense of foreboding emerges when we hear that jihadist forces have murdered Croatian construction workers nearby and are rumored to have the Catholic monks in their sights as the ultimate prize. The monks must now decide what to do. Should they stay or should they go? Is going cowardice? Is staying arrogance? Is martyrdom their destiny? They agree to stay and begin to prepare themselves for what will undoubtedly be a grisly end.

*Of Gods and Men* climaxes in a quite incredible "Last Supper" sequence, in which the monks share red wine to the accompaniment of Tchaikovsky's "Grand Theme" from *Swan Lake*, playing on an old tape machine in the corner. Indeed, on several occasions we have seen the monks refuse to interrupt their worship when it looks as though jihadist attack is imminent, but this scene is their final meal together and Beauvois' camera pans slowly around the table throughout, focusing briefly on each man's careworn face as he absorbs the mystery of his own death. It is an overwhelming fusion of portraiture and drama. It is apparent that the monks love their lives, but they love God more, and the camaraderie over wine and a simple meal must be seen in this context. This extraordinary piece of film is a depiction of rightly ordered loves and is an affront to the self-centered, excarnate world we find ourselves in. Like the Moravians singing below decks or the Cistercians setting the meal table, we must learn to integrate our desires in action with the ultimate priority of loving God and hungering for his righteousness. This ought not lead us away from engagement in the world or with each other—like some cosmic contemporary worship service, our hands aloft, our brows furrowed in ecstatic personal concentration—but into an awareness of the utter sacredness of life and action and service and love and food and laughter and worship and wine. Our liturgical life and our habits shape and reorder our desires.

French philosopher Pierre Teilhard de Chardin was expressing

the same in the 1960s, particularly in this beautifully phrased
passage from *Hymn of the Universe*:

> Let us ponder over this basic truth until we are steeped in
> it, until it becomes as familiar to us as our awareness of
> shapes or our reading of words: God, at his most vitally
> active and most incarnate, is not remote from us, wholly
> apart from the sphere of the tangible; on the contrary, at
> every moment he awaits us in the activity, the work to be
> done, which every moment brings. He is, in a sense, at the
> point of my pen, my pick, my paint-brush, my needle—and
> my heart and my thought. It is by carrying to its natural
> completion the stroke, the line, the stitch I am working on
> that I shall lay hold on that ultimate end towards which my
> will at its deepest levels tends.[1]

And yet half a century has passed since he wrote those words and
the church seems still to be uninterested in helping its members
find the presence of God in the practices of writing, hoeing, painting
or sewing, nor to help them express their faith bodily as they so do.
I think the answer is, as Smith points out, an acknowledgment of
the fact that our ultimate love is revealed by what we worship, and
when we foster lifestyles with godly habits and practices God becomes the ultimate object of our love. Other pursuits or endeavors
are not necessarily to be denied or abandoned, but rightly ordered.
As Tim Keller sums up, "Sin isn't only doing bad things, it is more
fundamentally making good things into ultimate things."[2] In this
respect, writing, hoeing, painting or sewing are potentially godly
expressions of true worship when ordered properly under God's
prior claim to our allegiance. Some churches of a more dualistic
persuasion make this an either-or issue: *either* we worship God *or*
we worship our own pursuits. This often ends up looking like *either*
we go to church *or* we shovel snow or picnic with friends or watch

the game on television. We are forced to choose between God and other perfectly healthy and acceptable pursuits.

Surely, a more integrated approach is to say that when we worship and love God as our priority, then we can sense him at the point of our pens or our paintbrushes and needles or in shoveling snow, picnicking or enjoying sports. We don't have to give up behaviors that are not sinful, we infuse them with Godward direction, and in carrying them out we are working toward ultimate ends. Furthermore, though, we also need to develop a rhythm of practices, liturgies and habits—both privately and in community—that can punctuate our lives and provide a kind of habitual scaffolding to assist us in maintaining rightly ordered loves. As Simone Weil is quoted as saying,

> One has only the choice between God and idolatry. If one denies God . . . one is worshiping some things of this world in the belief that one sees them only as such, but in fact, though unknown to oneself imagining the attributes of Divinity in them.[3]

## DESTRUCTIVE GOD SUBSTITUTES

In *The Reason for God*, Tim Keller defines sin as "building your identity on anything other than God." He takes this from Søren Kierkegaard's *The Sickness Unto Death*, in which the Danish philosopher categorizes sinfulness as the search for "god-substitutes." Keller explains that speaking to people about sin is simply revealing the damage and brokenness such substitutes bring to their lives. Instead of telling them they are sinning because they are sleeping around, he tells them that they are sinning because they are looking to their careers and romances to save them, to give them everything that they should be looking for in God. This idolatry leads to drivenness, addictions, severe anxiety, obsessiveness, envy of others and resentment. He then goes on to outline the ways in which wrongly ordered loves lead to such destruction by exploring the repercussions of such god substitutes:

- If you center your life and identity on your spouse or partner, you will be emotionally dependent, jealous and controlling. The other person's problems will be overwhelming to you.

- If you center your life and identity on your family and children, you will try to live your life through your children until they resent you or have no self of their own. At worst, you may abuse them when they displease you.

- If you center your life and identity on your work and career, you will be a driven workaholic and a boring, shallow person. At worst you will lose family and friends and, if your career goes poorly, develop depression.

- If you center your life and identity on money and possessions, you'll be eaten up by worry or jealousy about money. You'll be willing to do unethical things to maintain your lifestyle, which will eventually blow up your life.

- If you center your life and identity on pleasure, gratification and comfort, you will find yourself getting addicted to something. You will become chained to the "escape strategies" by which you avoid the hardness of life.

- If you center your life and identity on relationships and approval, you will be constantly overly hurt by criticism and thus always losing friends. You will fear confronting others and therefore be a useless friend.

- If you center your life and identity on a "noble cause," you will divide the world into "good" and "bad" and demonize your opponents. Ironically, you will be controlled by your enemies. Without them you will have no purpose.

- If you center your life and identity on religion and morality, you will, if you are living up to your moral standards, be proud, self-righteous and cruel. If you don't live up to your standards, your guilt will be utterly devastating.[4]

While possibly a bit too predictive, Keller's point is well made nonetheless and takes us back to James K. A. Smith's original suggestion that what we love we worship. If, however, what we love is not God, not only will we worship it, we will be led astray by it.

Coming back to Augustine, we do well to remember his old maxim: "You made us for yourself, and our hearts are restless until we find our rest in you." And taking Keller's last point, even if that god substitute is religion, it will take you to a very unhappy place. This raises the question as to whether a great deal of what is dished up in many churches every week is actually a destructive form of religion that, rather than helping congregational members rightly order their loves under their ultimate allegiance for God, in fact reinforces an excarnate faith that insists on institutional religious practices over everyday expressions of life and worship. In this respect, even church membership can then become a destructive god substitute.

Many of us can think of people we've met in churches who love serving on boards more than they love God. Then there are those who love the church building more than they love God. In both cases their wrongly ordered love has made them, as Keller says, proud, self-righteous and at times cruel. This isn't to say that loving boards or buildings is necessarily ungodly, any more than loving anything on Keller's list—spouses, children, career, possessions, pleasure, friends, causes or morality—is necessarily ungodly. But when they become substitutes for God, they become idolatrous. A truly incarnated theology allows believers to embody their devotion to God in everyday acts, to see all good and noble pursuits as or-

dered under the preeminence of God. The excarnate version traps
our devotion to God in overtly religious practices that may or may
not be expressions of God's preeminence. What's more, nowadays
philosophers like Alain de Botton have concluded that the external
trappings of the religious life are quite legitimate in and of themselves with no need for faith to sustain them. In *Religion for Atheists*,
de Botton, himself an atheist, argues that the supernatural claims
of religion are entirely false, and yet religions still have some very
important things to teach the secular world. In fact, says de Botton,
atheists should steal all the good ideas taught by religions on how
we might live and arrange our societies. Blending grudging respect,
a somewhat patronizing tone and total impiety, he proposes that we
should look to religions for insights into, among other concerns,
how to

- build a sense of community

- make our relationships last

- overcome feelings of envy and inadequacy

- escape the twenty-four-hour media

- go traveling

- get more out of art, architecture and music

- create new businesses designed to address our emotional needs[5]

Here's how to enjoy the range of consoling and beautiful rituals and
ideas present in the religious life without having to swallow doc-
trines or acknowledge the universal reign of God through Christ.
And yet, as shocking as that might sound to the faithful among us,
is it not essentially the same approach that many Christians take?
Religious practice, no matter how noble, without a preeminent love
for God is as potentially destructive as Tim Keller suggests. For too
many excarnate Christians, de Botton's hollow atheistic ode to religion sounds like gospel truth.

## A THEOLOGY OF PERSONS

The third broad contribution I want to explore is the development of a Christian theology of human persons. We seem to be happy to have swallowed whole a kind of Neo-Platonic bifurcation of the self without any reflection on whether this is a truly Christian understanding of persons. Alan Hirsch has helped us greatly with his exploration of the Hebraic worldview and its emphasis on human holism as distinct from the Greco-Roman dualism still so prevalent today.[6] Even more challenging work in this area has been done recently by Fuller Seminary professor Nancey Murphy. In *Bodies and Souls, or Spirited Bodies?* Murphy points out that there has been something like 130 different views of the human person, although she says that people tend to find themselves in one of four broad categories. First, there's physicalism, whose adherents believe that humans are composed of one part—a physical body. It can be assumed that most biologists and especially neuroscientists are physicalists. Secular philosophers are almost all physicalists as well.

The second option is dualism, which Murphy breaks into two versions: (1) body-soul dualism and (2) body-mind dualism, the former having religious connotations that the latter has not. I suggest dualism is the most popular view, both in the church and beyond.

A third theory is called trichotomism. This view comes from Paul's blessing in 1 Thessalonians 5:23: "May the God of peace himself sanctify you entirely; and may your spirit and soul and body be kept blameless at the coming of the Lord Jesus Christ" (NRSV). Trichotomists hold that humans are composed of three parts: body, soul and spirit.

Murphy writes that she regularly conducts research with her students on where they would place themselves and has found that among evangelical students at Fuller, as well as with her more general audiences at conferences and the like, dualism and trichotomism compete for first place. She also concludes, "Christian philosophers are divided between dualism and physicalism. When I speak at seminaries on the liberal end of the spectrum all but incoming students are physicalists. At more conservative institutions faculty members are split between dualism and physicalism."[7]

A fourth option—idealism—holds that humans are composed of one part—a spiritual/mental substance. This view is popular among New Age thinkers. Murphy gives it short shrift.

Ultimately, Murphy rejects all four options as being inadequate explanations of the breadth of biblical perspectives on persons. She contends that the popularity of dualistic or trichotomistic views among evangelicals and other conservative Christians has been made possible because "the Bible has no clear teaching here. This has made it possible for Christians in different eras to recognize a variety of views in the texts, and, perhaps more importantly, to have read a variety of views into the texts."[8] Before readers react to that statement, she is not suggesting that the Bible doesn't talk about bodies and souls and spirits. We just noted Paul's reference to all three in 1 Thessalonians 5. Instead, Murphy is saying that nowhere in Scripture do the biblical authors offer clear, unequivocal definitions of terms like *soul*, *psyche* and *spirit*, and neither can we find a full treatment of their relationship within the human person. Murphy argues for a modified version of physicalism, acknowledging that the scientific understanding of physicalism has a number of philosophical problems that need to be addressed if it is to be acceptable to Christians. She develops the idea of spirited bodies as a kind of physicalist alternative to the dualism of bodies and souls: "We are, at our best, complex physical organisms, imbued with the legacy of thousands of years of culture, and, most importantly, blown by the Breath of God's Spirit; *we are Spirited Bodies*."[9]

The distinction between "spirited bodies" and dualism is a subtle one, as best as I can understand it, but I nonetheless take Murphy's

general thrust that the church has largely embraced an overly developed dualism that has proven to be unhelpful and has given religious endorsement to the excarnational forces in secular society.
Rowan Williams, the former archbishop of Canterbury, addresses
a similar concern with an overdeveloped sense of the human "self."
Rejecting the dichotomy between an "inner identity" and an "outer
identity" he says:

> Common to a good deal of contemporary philosophical re-
> flection on human identity is the conviction that we are system-
> atically misled, even corrupted, by a picture of the human agent
> as divided into an outside and an inside—a "true self," hidden,
> buried, to be excavated by one or another kind of therapy.[10]

He believes this "self" is a morally problematic fiction. It suggests
that my deepest interests are individual and preordained, and this
idea undermines any notion that the human situation fundamentally embodies a common task. For Williams there is no complete,
a priori identity to be unearthed by peeling away various layers of
outer existence; rather, the real self is found or made from the very
beginning in human communication and interaction. Williams
does not deny interiority—believing that it emerges from the hard
work of human engagement—but he does suggest that a rhetoric of
interiority has had serious moral and cultural consequences. These
consequences are picked up by Philip Sheldrake in his challenge
article "Christian Spirituality as a Way of Living Publicly." His
thesis is a theological antidote to the defleshing tendencies of
secular life. After unraveling the interior-exterior dualism we have
just been discussing—citing Meister Eckhart, Evelyn Underhill,
David Tracey, Leonardo Boff and Jürgen Moltmann as evidence—he
argues powerfully for an understanding of Christian spirituality as
a vital ingredient in our engagement with transformative practice
in the outer, public world. He says,

I do not believe that we need to discard interiority in favor of radical exteriority. This merely perpetuates an unhelpful dichotomy in another guise. Interiority and exteriority express complementary dimensions of human life that should be held in dialectical tension.[11]

This tension, however, must result in a heightened capacity for the Christian to "live publicly." Indeed, he goes so far as to say the only spirituality worthy of being termed Christian must result in action in the public sphere. He says that even those authors best known for a mysticism heavy on invitations to retreat and contemplation take a much more engaged or public orientation than we give them credit for:

Mysticism has often been interpreted as the most radically inward form of Christian spirituality, yet the classic mystical texts, properly understood, do not support the viewpoint that mysticism is a "tropical luxuriance" with no role in public, political life. As Evelyn Underhill suggests in her classic book *Mysticism*, a defining characteristic of Christian mysticism is that union with God impels a person towards an active, outward, rather than purely passive, inward life.[12]

Murphy's phrase *spirited bodies* is helpful here. As spirited bodies we are invited to a rich and dynamic union with God through Christ, but such a union must always result in an impulse to join God in the public sphere. We are our bodies, nonetheless, while "spirited" by our connection to God.

As suggested by the title of his work, Sheldrake prefers to see Christian spirituality being expressed chiefly in public life.

To live publicly means letting go of a life focused on the survival of the autonomous self. It involves engaging the other in ways that embrace diversity as part of the process of establishing and reinforcing the self. Living publicly implies real encounters, learning how to be truly hospitable to what is different and unfamiliar, and establishing and experiencing a common life. Living publicly excludes social or political quietism, it excludes existing passively in the midst of the world. Interaction, participation, and active citizenship thus should be seen as forms of spiritual practice.[13]

Such a vision of spiritual practice is possible when we see all human longing as God-directed, when we understand that our desires are not all evil but need to be rightly ordered. Then our interactions with others are not seen as time away from God but time spent with him. Our participation in community service, sports, the arts and business are perceived as potentially sacred activities. However, the trick is to assist Christians in developing a rhythm of life that values contemplation, reflection and prayer (as interior work) as well as living publicly as a spiritual practice. While James K. A. Smith looks to liturgy and worship for the answer, I want to broaden that discussion to include missional practices and daily habits. I will explore this further in chapter nine, but the following is a simple example of what this might look like.

### SPIRITED INCARNATIONAL PRAYER

Some years ago a friend introduced me to a prayer cycle based on the five prayers recorded in Luke 1–2. Each prayer is recited at a certain time in the day, which offers a way of reflecting spiritually on the story of Christ, while being propelled into action in the public sphere. The cycle goes like this:

*Upon rising.*
I am the Lord's servant. . . . May your word to me be fulfilled. (Luke 1:38)

By echoing Mary's prayer of resignation and obedience, we begin our day with expectancy and faithfulness. This prayer readies us to accept whatever the Lord brings that day, as obediently as Mary accepted her vocation as the mother of Christ. It launches us into the public work where we spend most of our days. It can be prayed kneeling or with open hands to physically express submission and humility.

> *Morning.*
> My soul glorifies the Lord
>     and my spirit rejoices in God my Savior,
> for he has been mindful
>     of the humble state of his servant.
> From now on all generations will call me blessed,
>     for the Mighty One has done great things for me—
>     holy is his name.
> His mercy extends to those who fear him,
>     from generation to generation.
> He has performed mighty deeds with his arm;
>     he has scattered those who are proud in their inmost
>         thoughts.
> He has brought down rulers from their thrones
>     but has lifted up the humble.
> He has filled the hungry with good things
>     but has sent the rich away empty.
> He has helped his servant Israel,
>     remembering to be merciful
> to Abraham and his descendants forever,
>     just as he promised our ancestors. (Lk 1:46-55)

Praying the Magnificat at our desk as a daily pause in the midst of what is often the busiest part of the day acknowledges God's grand design and how it dwarfs whatever "important" work has occupied our attention. Praying it daily sets our own work in the context of God's work of setting everything right in the world. It infuses our work with ultimate meaning while recognizing the puniness of that work in the scheme of things.

*Midday*.
Praise be to the Lord, the God of Israel,
  because he has come to his people and redeemed them.
He has raised up a horn of salvation for us
  in the house of his servant David
(as he said through his holy prophets of long ago),
    salvation from our enemies and from the hand of all who
      hate us—
to show mercy to our ancestors
  and to remember his holy covenant,
  the oath he swore to our father Abraham:
to rescue us from the hand of our enemies,
  and to enable us to serve him without fear
  in holiness and righteousness before him all our days.
    (Luke 1:68-75)

Zechariah's Benedictus forms the perfect punctuation point in the middle of the day. It is a prayer of thankfulness for God's mercy to us in his Son, Jesus. By praying it before lunch every day we "re-gospel" ourselves afresh.

*Afternoon*.
Glory to God in the highest heaven,
  and on earth peace to those on whom his favor rests.
    (Luke 2:14)

The prayer of the triumphant angels on the hills outside Bethlehem is the simplest and most beautiful announcement of the lordship of God. It declares that he reigns utterly, totally and completely. My friend says he leaves his downtown office and pauses on the street, looking up at the billboards and the neon names of the city's largest corporations, all clambering for preeminence over the business district. He quietly looks skyward, raises his hands and repeats the angels' prayer, acknowledging that God is above all.

*Evening.*
Sovereign Lord, as you have promised,
    you may now dismiss your servant in peace.
For my eyes have seen your salvation,
    which you have prepared in the sight of all nations:
a light for revelation to the Gentiles,
    and the glory of your people Israel. (Luke 2:29-32)

When Simeon first prayed this, the dismissal he spoke of was the end of his own life, but we can appropriate the prayer as an expression of our evening dismissal, as we lay our heads upon our pillows.

For Ignatius of Loyola a "spiritual exercise" was anything that prepares us to receive the grace of God. If we perceive spiritual exercises to be limited to explicitly personal and private religious practices, there is a problem for those who desire to remain profoundly engaged with the public world. Such a belief only reinforces the excarnate understanding of God operating only—or primarily—in our inner worlds. Maintaining a prayer rhythm in the midst of life is one answer. But it's not the only one. As mentioned in chapter seven and reiterated by C. S. Lewis earlier, we need to also cultivate an attentiveness that focuses on God's self-disclosure in all things. As Philip Sheldrake concludes,

Every moment, every action is a potential context for movements of God's spirit to be experienced, for resistances to be overcome, for discernment to take place, for life-directing choices to be made, for commitment to God to be deepened. In this way our outer, public activities may be transformed into a genuine spiritual exercise.[14]

# 9

# Mission in the Excarnate Age

*Christian life is not a life divided between*
*times for action and times for contemplation. No.*
*Real social action is a way of contemplation, and real*
*contemplation is the core of social action.*

HENRI NOUWEN

⌐⌐

**Given the excarnate impulses on Christian faith** and thinking, is it any wonder that the outworking of such should result in increasingly defleshed approaches to mission? I suggest we are seeing this work itself out in (1) the explosion of online activism in preference for the embodied service of others, (2) an ever-widening gap in the church-world dualism, and (3) approaches to evangelism that appeal to highly individualized and internalized decisions to follow Christ. In all three cases we are being pulled away from the Christian ideal of mission being rooted in a community of humble men and women who truly believe the gospel and practice it in the lives of those around them. We resist these excarnational forces and come closer to the mission God has for us when we intentionally root ourselves in a messy, organic, missional community of faith. Here, we serve the poor and house the homeless and enter meaningfully into the lives of those around us as an incarnational witness to the goodness of God in Christ.

## THE RISE OF CLICK ACTIVISM

In 2011, after the tragic sinking of several boats carrying asylum seekers from Indonesia to Australia, a Sydney-based men's magazine, *Zoo Weekly*, decided to cash in on the story in the most debasing way. First, the magazine, which specializes in smutty images of big breasted models in bikinis, offered to house the next boatload of asylum seekers in its office if a young female senator, Sarah Hanson-Young, agreed to appear in a "tasteful" bikini or lingerie shoot. Ms. Hanson-Young, a noted supporter of more lenient immigration policies toward refugees, ignored the tasteless offer. In response, *Zoo Weekly* photoshopped her face onto the body of a busty, scantily clad model in their next edition.

As if that were not bad enough, the magazine then ran an outrageous competition to find "Australia's hottest asylum seeker" with the following call out:

> Are you a refugee not even the immigration minister could refuse? Then we want to see you! We're looking for Oz's hottest asylum seeker, so if you've swapped persecution for sexiness, we want to shoot you (with a camera—relax!) Send your pics and a short story about your tragic past.

The accompanying double-page spread featured images of buxom models on a luxury yacht, presumably simulating "hot asylum seekers." One busty blond is portrayed with a speech bubble saying, "We could be assets to this country." Her equally voluptuous friend replies, "Yes, big assets."

In response to this crass and juvenile publicity stunt, refugee-support worker Matt Darvas unloaded on the activist website Change.org, which allows people to start petitions, garner public outrage and effect change. He launched a petition to have *Zoo Weekly* abandon their proposed photo shoot, writing,

> I live amongst and count as close friends a number of female refugees from several war-torn nations in East Africa. They still suffer symptoms of post-traumatic stress, including frequent nightmares, flashbacks, depression and other associated health problems. To trivialize and exploit these incredibly traumatic experiences is utterly appalling. That's why I'm calling on [*Zoo Weekly*'s publisher] ACP Magazines to demand *Zoo* issue an apology and immediately scrap this disgusting competition.

The petition attracted 6,500 signatures and was reported in the international press, including the *Guardian* in the UK, shaming *Zoo Weekly* into a retraction of the competition and an apology for any offense caused to their readers, to any asylum seeker or refugee and their families and supporters, and to Senator Sarah Hanson-Young.

It could be suggested that *Zoo Weekly* got all the free publicity they wanted during that sorry incident, but I agree with Matt Darvas that it would have been unconscionable for the Christian community to have done nothing in the face of this kind of public humiliation of refugees and the trivializing of a deeply concerning situation where asylum seekers brave shark-infested waters in leaky boats to find freedom in the West, with one in every twenty-five boat people dying in the process. Chalk one up for the forces of good over evil.

But the nature of Darvas's victory is a telling one. His championing of the rights of asylum seekers was supported by thousands of people who have never actually met a refugee in their life. While Matt Darvas himself has supported and worked with refugees for a number of years, his campaign would never have been a success were it not for the click activism of many others who have not. Surely this is a classic example of excarnate social action. I am not being critical of Darvas's campaign, nor of the 6,500 people who supported it. Indeed, I was one of them. And I am very much aware of the important uses of the Internet for Christian mission in getting the word out, recruiting supporters, increasing the visibility of our cause, and nudging people toward greater interest and involvement. I am nonetheless pointing out the ease with which people today can join a campaign or support a cause with absolutely no personal or physical investment in the matter whatsoever.

Disparagingly also called "slacktivism," click activism is becoming a monumental global trend, but is it really achieving very much (the *Zoo Weekly* campaign aside)? And is it simply another example of the excarnate reality we as Christians need to resist? With the emergence of many point-and-click Christian campaigns, as well as the growing popularity of short-term mission trips and short-term advocacy campaigns, it is worth asking whether even the mission of the church is becoming excarnate. When the extent of our commitment to a cause can be reduced to pointing and clicking, have we become too beholden to excarnate forms of caring? Jimmy Kimmel commented on the recent trend of people changing their Facebook profile photos to the red equal sign in support of same-sex marriage. "It is literally the least you can do," Kimmel said. "You almost did nothing, but instead you did just slightly more than nothing."

Of course, click activism has an obvious and understandable appeal. It is convenient and, in some cases like the *Zoo Weekly* campaign, it can be effective. It can also be a satisfying way for people to express their feelings of outrage or injustice at certain issues. There's a sense of immediacy and participation located in online campaigns. The clickers not only get to give expression to their feelings but also have a sense they are doing something, no matter how small, about the matter at hand. So it can be efficacious, and it's certainly personally satisfying. And not all activism is local. So changing your Twitter location to Tehran, for example, is a symbolic exercise in solidarity with protestors against the Iranian government. It's a way that I, stuck in Sydney, can participate in a struggle thousands of miles away. Likewise with many other online forms of advocacy. And, of course, many of the people who are clicking and reposting are themselves genuine activists. Their virtual activism is an extension, not a replacement, of their real activism. Furthermore, the virtual world is itself terrain. So, occupying it and controlling it is an act of resistance. The same day those millions of people changed their Facebook profiles to Tehran, a few thousand teachers and their sympathizers protested in the streets of Chicago. The terrain of the former was much more visible than the latter, bringing much greater pressure to bear on the situation as a result. All that being said, it's the lazy, barely engaged use of online activism—slacktivism—I'm concerned about.

I recently happened upon a website called the Lazy Activist (www.lazyactivist.com), boasting to offer "the easiest activism on the Net." Reflect on that name for just a minute. The lazy activist. It makes no real sense, does it? Basically, the site has been established as a one-stop shop for all point-and-click campaigns in the United States. The home page introduces the site this way:

> The Lazy Activist is designed to encourage *EVERYONE*, including *YOU* and everyone you know, to become an activist quickly and easily by using the Internet. The Internet has made it easier than ever to get informed, to get involved and to get others involved.
>
> The Lazy Activist gets you to sites that allow you to learn more about the issues and take ACTION in a matter of seconds. Great news! Most of the sites The Lazy Activist includes are free, too! So take action today, even if it's just one click!
>
> Use The Lazy Activist to take action in the United States. Use the Issue Specific Links page for activism resources worldwide.

The Lazy Activist then offers links to other activist sites run by such groups as MoveOn, People for the American Way, Amnesty, PETA, EarthJustice, the Sierra Club and the Hunger Site, where visitors can click to sign petitions, express support, post links to Facebook or even to donate food to the hungry. Now, again, I'm not questioning the sincerity of those who participate in click activism. They are often driven by a very genuine desire to help or to express their outrage at a certain injustice. The deeper question I want to ask is whether activist sites actually make it easier for us not to actively engage in real, physical ways, in the causes that move us. Admittedly, we can't all get physically involved everywhere, and the Internet does afford us the opportunity to support causes that would otherwise be well beyond our ability to access. However, I would argue that when click activism becomes our primary (or even solo) engagement with social need, we are drifting into dangerous excarnate territory. As much as we might need to sign an online petition, we also need to welcome people into our homes, to share food at our tables. We also need to cross the street or cross an ocean and move into the neighborhood to bring the peace and justice and mercy of Christ into clearer sight for those who suffer. The thousands of likes on the Facebook page for the ONE campaign haven't solved the world's hunger problem.

Mocking click activism, Adbusters contributing editor Micah White remarked drolly,

> I am a digital native, a member of the first generation to be born surrounded by computers. So when my generation was called to stop the impending war against Iraq, I joined together with my friends and did the one thing we trusted would be most effective: *we built a great looking website.*[1]

As funny as that sounds, White goes on to say that he and his friends actually thought a great looking website would really change the course of history. In spite of attracting twenty thousand visitors a month, their website made no difference to the prosecution of the Iraq War. That was because revolutionary change only occurs when men and women believe something to be true and act on it in bodily, socially construed ways. In other words, there needs to be a transformation of human nature and a willingness to physically act before there can be a transformation of human society. White continues,

> Posting spoofs of Nike on YouTube, podcasting about politics from a bedroom or using text messaging to organize protests are uses of technology that alter social relations and consequently human nature. However, the question remains whether the changes . . . that the Internet is bringing about will allow us to usher in a positively transformed world. I believe the answer is no because the essential experience of the Internet, even at its most interactive, is of solitary individuals mediating all of their passion through a screen. If we want a world with strong communities able to fend off the intrusions of mega-corporations, diverse local culture that varies from place to place and neighborhoods with neighbors who know each other enough to feel safe at home, then the paradigm of the Internet is leading us astray.

## KONY 2012

Nowhere has this been more apparent than the recent Kony 2012 campaign. Produced by US-based charity Invisible Children, *Kony 2012* was a short film released on the Internet in March 2012 with the expressed purpose of making Ugandan cult and militia leader, indicted war criminal and International Criminal Court fugitive Joseph Kony globally known in order to have him arrested by the end of 2012, when the campaign expired. Within a month of its release *Kony 2012* had over 100 million views on YouTube and

Vimeo. It was estimated that more than half of young adult Americans heard about *Kony 2012* in the days following the film's release. Its impact was global. It has been the biggest point-and-click activist campaign in history. So, how did Invisible Children manage to generate such a remarkable response to their campaign? There are several reasons:

1. *High production values.* It was a professionally produced film with high-level use of After Effects, slick editing and excellent integration of Facebook and other social media.

2. *An emotional plea made with great conviction and energy.* A minute-and-a-half in, filmmaker Jason Russell says, "The next twenty-seven minutes are an experiment, but in order for it to work, you have to pay attention." It's riveting. But more than that, through the manipulative use of emotion, particular by the appearance of Russell's small son, every single line did what it was designed to do—elicit emotional outrage in its viewers.

3. *A powerful appeal to the viewer's ego.* The early section of the film is all about the power of social media and the ability of its young adult users to change the world. Sections of the film focus on Jacob, a Ugandan teenager who appeals to the video's audience—Western teenagers. Teens helping teens makes the cause a generational issue, not a race/religion/nationality issue, although it could be suggested that the film appeals to Americans in particular and their global burden to help the world's poor.

4. *A simple solution to a complex problem.* Kony 2012 offers a very straightforward solution to the terribly complex situation in Uganda: Step 1. Raise awareness about Kony. Step 2. Arrest Kony. And do it all by a clear deadline, December 31, 2012. The campaign projected the belief that there was no need for a long commitment to a tedious, ongoing cause. More than that, it takes what might otherwise seem like a depressingly hopeless subject and makes it entertaining and watchable. Indeed, the horrendous things that Joseph Kony makes

his child soldiers do is entirely unsuitable for general viewing, but *Kony 2012* appeals to the typical PG-13 audience. As a result, the viewer gets it without having to be traumatized.

5. *The creation of an activist brand.* Invisible Children makes such things as signing pledges, buying promotional kits and sharing the video as easy as possible, thanks to a website that features prewritten letters to Members of Congress, social media buttons and so forth. Their Action Kit made advocacy fun, simple and rewarding. Their T-shirts and posters were hip, well designed and just cheap enough for anyone to afford. And by employing the promotional talents of a band of celebrities like Bono, Stephen Colbert, Justin Bieber and Angelina Jolie, they reinforced the hip nature of their brand.

And yet despite the extraordinary success of the March release of *Kony 2012*, the short attention spans and general cynicism of their intended audience became their undoing. When aid agencies began asking for more information on their campaign, Invisible Children felt compelled to release a follow-up film, *Kony 2012: Part II—Beyond Famous*. It was said to offer a more solid, moving and ultimately accurate presentation of the ongoing battle to capture Joseph Kony. However, Mike Pflanz, East Africa correspondent for the *Daily Telegraph*, said the "new video is couched in nuance and deploys dialogue more commonly heard in a United Nations workshop—displacement, rehabilitation, post-conflict—than in a YouTube smash."[2] And therein lies the reason for its limited success. According to the *Guardian*, the sequel "does not seem to have captured the public's imagination in quite the same way as Invisible Children's earlier video did, failing to significantly trend on social media websites."[3] By April 16, 2012, it had received 1.7 million views in eleven days, less than 2 percent of what the first video had in its first five days. The audience had moved on. The Kony phenomenon had run out of steam within a month of its launch. By the end of 2012, Joseph Kony was still free.

Aside from the unique mistakes made by Invisible Children's campaign, *Kony 2012* is a prime example of the nature of excarnate campaigns in general. They don't seem to affect very great change in the world. And my fear is that after an American teen has been involved in two or three of them, he or she is in great danger of sliding into utter cynicism about their capacity to make any difference to anyone at all. In other words, click activism might be developing a less idealistic and altruistic generation than we had ever imagined. Micah White concludes:

> Internet based activism is a retreat from the local struggles of everyday life; it is a flight from our concrete streets to the fiber-optic superhighway. As such, Internet campaigning imparts the worst lesson of all: it teaches a generation of activists to forgo picking up struggles around them in favor of distant battles they have the least ability to impact. As Simon Critchley writes, "resistance begins by occupying and controlling the terrain upon which one stands, where one lives, works, acts and thinks."[4]

Occupying such terrain is essential to fashioning meaningful change. And while I in no way want to suggest Christians are merely sitting at home clicking away on their favorite websites and doing nothing practical where they live, work, act and think, we do need to be cautious about the degree to which lazy activism is dominating the church's missional agenda.

## VACATIONARIES AND VOLUNTOURISTS

Not only has the Internet changed the landscape of social activism and Christian mission, we've also seen the rise in the popularity of short-term mission (STM) trips, through which Christians can participate on a part-time basis as "vacationaries." They are a vexed question in the field of missiology. Supporters of STMs claim they give people a taste of an overseas missions experience, enough to lead them to consider longer term service in the future. Alternatively, they say, a STM can foster in participants a commitment to missionary service that will motivate them to promote missions in their home churches. On the other hand, many people wish such trips did not exist, at least in the common form today. Writing in his book *Toxic Charity*, Robert Lupton says, "Contrary to popular belief, most missions trips and service projects do not: empower those being served, engender healthy cross-cultural relationships, improve quality of lives, relieve poverty, change the lives of participants [or] increase support for long-term missions work."[5]

Recently we've also seen the emergence of "voluntourism" across the world. Whether it's working with children in orphanages, helping to build houses or teaching English, so-called voluntourism is a fast-growing sector of the travel industry. Orphanage tourism is now prevalent across Southeast Asia. In north Thailand, especially around Chiang Mai, numerous orphanages are populated by the children from Thailand's ethnic minority hill tribes, long the most disadvantaged people in Thai society. A number of orphanages in south Thailand charge up to $400 a week for volunteers to spend time with children supposedly orphaned by the devastating 2004 tsunami.

At its most basic, it can mean visiting an orphanage for a few hours as part of scheduled tour that also involves more conventional activities such as sightseeing. Some people, though, choose to spend longer periods volunteering in orphanages, paying for the opportunity to play and read with the children or teaching them English. Of course many tourists find the experience highly emotive and uplifting, life-changing in some cases, while even those who visit for only a few hours can feel that their donations will make a difference to the lives of the orphans. But for many aid organizations, orphanage tourism is an unwelcome phenomenon, one that turns the most vulnerable members of society into mere tourist attractions. Ngo Menghourng, the Cambodia communications officer for the NGO Friends International, says, "Ask yourself whether a similar situation would be allowed in your own country: busloads of tourists pouring into a children's home for fleeting visits, being allowed to interact with and photograph the children? No it wouldn't."[6]

UNICEF recently launched a campaign to stop orphanage tourism in Cambodia. Ngo Menghourng says, "Orphanage tourism lays children open to exploitation, puts them at risk through unregulated visitation and fuels bad practise in relation to residential care for children."[7]

But of course orphanage visits are also a very common part of a short-term mission trip these days. I suspect that's because orphanages are full of smiling kids who respond with great joy when Westerners appear bearing gifts and offering to play games with them. Helping out an orphanage for a day is a doable, manageable enterprise, whereas genuinely seeking to address the causes of chronic poverty and corruption in Developing World countries is certainly not a short-term project.

In *Toxic Charity* Robert Lupton affirms the mindset that compels Christians toward foreign short-term missions and inner-city projects at home, but believes that the church has failed to ask simple questions about who is really benefiting from all this short-term activity. Indeed, he says it has caused great harm. Drawing on four decades of urban ministry, primarily in poverty-stricken areas of Atlanta, Lupton offers a better way forward in the form of an "Oath for Compassionate Service," a missions equivalent to the doctor's Hippocratic Oath.

• Never do for the poor what they have (or could have) the capacity to do for themselves.

- Limit one-way giving to emergency situations.

- Strive to empower the poor through employment, lending, and investing, using grants sparingly to reinforce achievements.

- Subordinate self-interests to the needs of those being served. Listen closely to those you seek to help, especially to what is not being said—unspoken feelings may contain essential clues to effective service.

- Above all, do no harm.[8]

Like Lupton, I too want to affirm the impulse that drives Christians to undertake short-term trips or build websites or sign online petitions. That impulse is a good one. It comes from a real desire to help, to make a difference and to give expression to the love of God. But I also want to sound a warning that if orphanage visits or click activism is *all* we do, we have given in to the inexorable drift toward excarnation, when what the world so desperately needs are incarnational servants of Christ to wade into the muck and stench of this world and to partner with the locals, as broken as we all are, in helping to shape human society as God intended it to be.

# 10

# Defying Church-World Dualism

*A small body of determined spirits*
*fired by an unquenchable faith in their mission*
*can alter the course of history.*

MOHANDAS GANDHI

🔳

**Exacerbating disengagement in mission** is the entrenched dualism that continues to dog the church, chiefly the yawning gap promoted in churches between the Christian community and the world around them. I have said elsewhere that the simplest and most effective definition of the mission of God's people is that we are to alert everyone to the universal reign of God through Christ.[1] This will be done by both a verbal announcement of God's reign as well as a demonstration of the values and goodness of that reign under the noses of those who have not yet been set free. And so the mission of God's people, for example, can include both evangelistic campaigns *and* online petitions aimed at ending sex trafficking. It can include personal witness *and* the practice of hospitality. But it must also include "occupying and controlling the terrain upon which one stands, where one lives, works, acts and thinks."[2] The mission of God's people must involve alerting people to the universal reign of God through Christ by their work, play, politics, business, arts, community service, education and so on. Indeed, I suggest it is an outworking of the excarnate impulses in society and the church that has allowed us to think that God's reign only extends as far as the Christian community and, more specifically, the hearts of individual Christians. Surely Christ's kingship extends over every sphere of human endeavor and indeed over the whole universe. By allowing ourselves to be marginalized within society as being "experts" in the so-called religious realm only, we have effectively left society to its own devices. And then we complained furiously when society moved away from our values. I suggest that if we take the reign of God seriously, we would be committed to equipping Christians to live out their faith incarnationally in every sphere of life. And yet we allow a kind of collective excarnation to take place, wherein God is present and pleased with us in church and when fulfilling church-based duties, but seemingly absent from the so-called profanity of everyday life.

In *Redeeming the Routines*, Robert Banks identifies the observable symptoms of this gap. When all our biblical teaching comes from (primarily) men who believe they are doing God's work, and that their congregants are doing some inferior kind of profane business, the likes of which they no longer remember or understand, we end up learning a curriculum that doesn't relate to our real life. As Banks points out, it's not just our employment that is irrelevant in the pulpit. So are our pastimes and hobbies, often berated as standing in the way of serving God, rather than being seen as means of doing so. As Banks says, the result is:

1. Few of us apply or know how to apply our belief to our work, or lack of work;

2. We only make minimal connections between our faith and our spare-time activities;

3. We have little sense of a Christian approach to regular activities like domestic chores;

4. Our everyday attitudes are partly shaped by the dominant values of our society;

5. Many of our spiritual difficulties stem from the daily pressure we experience (lack of time, exhaustion, family pressures, etc.);

6. Our everyday concerns receive little attention in the church;

7. Only occasionally do professional theologians address routine activities;

8. When addressed, everyday issues tend to be approached too theoretically;

9. Only a minority of Christians read religious books or attend theological courses;

10. Most churchgoers reject the idea of a gap between their beliefs and their ways of life.[3]

Study after study tells us that Christians feel they receive no help from their churches in how to live under the reign of God in every sphere of their life. Robert Banks quotes occasionally from an old book called *Christianity and Real Life*, written by William Diehl, the sales manager of a major steel corporation. Diehl writes about the gap between the secular and the sacred in church circles:

> In the almost thirty years of my professional career, my church has never once suggested that there be any type of accounting of my on-the-job ministry to others. My church has never once offered to improve those skills which could make me a better minister, nor has it ever asked if I needed any kind of support in what I was doing. There has never been an inquiry into the types of ethical decisions I must face, or whether I seek to communicate the faith to my coworkers. I have never

been in a congregation where there was any type of public affirmation of a ministry in my career. In short, I must conclude that my church really doesn't have the least interest whether or how I minister in my daily work.[4]

Diehl here is assuming that the only "ministry" he can perform at work is to share his faith with others, and even this isn't acknowledged or encouraged by his church. I want to suggest that there are even more fundamental ways we can mirror the work of God in our workplaces. But if the gap is as great as Diehl suggests, they are not ways the church seems at all ready for. We say we believe that God's reign is universal and complete, even if our appreciation of it is limited, veiled and mysterious. And still we participate in ways of being church that bolster the Neo-Platonic dualism that exacerbates the excarnate impulses seen in church life today. As Charles Ringma says,

> But no thought is given to establish what church members are already doing in their neighborhood and places of work. No attempt is made, for example, to identify the medical practitioner who has changed the approach to patients by providing counseling and practical support rather than just curative care. No attempt is made to identify the local [public official] in the congregation who is tackling certain important quality of life and social issues in the community. No attempt is made to support the lady who is conducting an informal neighborhood Bible study group. No attempt is made to support prayerfully the teacher who has just started work in an inner-city school with many pupils from broken families. And no attempt is made to see one family's care for their disabled child as a ministry worthy of the church's support and prayers.[5]

If the church today wishes to regain its place in Western culture and influence society for the glory of God, we need to recover a way of seeing God's reign as universal, and to equip every believer to submit to that reign in every sphere of life. This was Lesslie Newbigin's great quest toward the end of his life. Returning to England after decades as a missionary in southern India, he found the country of his birth more like a mission field than Madras. He set about catalyzing a conversation about how to re-Christianize a post-Christian culture. His prescription for this enormously difficult task is outlined in his book *Foolishness to the Greeks*, and I am prohibited from exploring all seven of his suggestions here. Suffice to say one of the important planks of his strategy was the "declericalizing" of the church and an equal rediscovery of the importance of so-called lay leaders who help congregations "to share with one another the actual experience of their weekday work and to seek illumination from the gospel for their daily secular duty."[6]

By seeking illumination from the gospel for their daily duty, Christians would be able to explore more fully what the universal reign of God through Christ looked like in their places of employment, their homes and neighborhoods. In this way the mission of God's people, which includes announcement and demonstration of the reign of God, could infiltrate every aspect of society, shifting culture slowly and surely toward the values of the gospel. As far as Newbigin was concerned, the reign of God is exercised over economics and business and the arts as much as it is over the church. Responding to the church's disinterest in matters of economics, for instance, he wrote, "Christians believed it was impossible to interfere with the workings of 'economic laws,' that the writ of Christ's kingship did not rein in the autonomous kingdom of economics, and that the best one could do was to offer charity to the victims."[7]

Far from it, he declared, Christ's kingship does indeed include economics, and the most fundamental way for the church to demonstrate that kingship is through the releasing of thousands of Christian economists, politicians, financiers and accountants to "seek illumination from the gospel for their daily secular duty." In so doing, a cultural tipping point could be reached which would see the West shift back toward a greater openness to the acknowledgment of God's reign through Christ. In saying this he was not advocating the emergence of some new Christian political movement that attempted to "reclaim" culture for Christ. This would have meant a return to the worst excesses of Christendom and, in every likelihood, would have not only failed but created great animosity from mainstream society. He saw a cultural tipping point being reached by the infiltration of every sphere of society by ordinary Christians who thought and acted "Christianly" in their everyday life. He wrote,

> If the gospel is to challenge the public life of our society, . . . it will not be by forming a Christian political party, or by aggressive propaganda campaigns. . . . It will only be by movements that begin with the local congregation in which the reality of the new creation is present, known and experienced.[8]

For a contemporary example of what this might look like, consider the effectiveness of gay activism over the past forty years. Rather than creating a formal pro-gay political party, the gay community effectively infiltrated every aspect of society, from business to politics to the arts. Their agenda was not to convert everyone to become homosexual, but to foster an increasingly gay-friendly society, and they have been spectacularly successful. Newbigin had something similar in mind. Instead of making the conversion of *every* person our goal, as if that was likely or ever even promised to us, what if we equipped every Christian to engage in every sphere of society to demonstrate the values of God's reign and rule? If that could be achieved, not only would it glorify God, it also could move

Western societies toward a cultural tipping point. Instead, we focus on a handful of hot-button issues like abortion or same-sex marriage and think that God's reign extends only to these areas. And in so doing, we have effectively abandoned the arts, the legal system, the education system, business and politics to the values of a post-Christian culture.

What I've been calling "spheres" Bob Roberts refers to as "domains" and suggests there are eight such domains in a global society: (1) economics, (2) agriculture, (3) education, (4) medical/science/technology, (5) communication, (6) arts and entertainment, (7) governance and justice, and (8) family.[9] These domains are evident on a national scale, in your state or province, and in your city. Depending on your geographic location, some domains are more prominent than others. Taking Roberts's list as a guide, what would it look like if we saw the mission of God's people to seek illumination from the gospel for their work in each of those areas? Remember that Newbigin advocated a declericalizing of the church. There's a story told of him that after he'd been accused of trying to eliminate the clergy, he shot back, "On the contrary, I am trying to eliminate the laity." By that he meant the declericalization of the church effectively means the ordination of every believer as an agent of the mission of God. It was his view that so-called lay leaders are the only ones who can help congregations seek illumination from the gospel for their daily secular duty. In other words, only a Christian filmmaker, doctor, lawyer or preschool teacher can know the actual experience of their workday, and they need like-minded people to workshop with them in exploring what the reign of God looks like in their particular context. The clergy can play the role of theological and biblical consultants in the process, but the church itself needs to explore what being a missional Christian looks like in any given circumstance.

As a mature Christian leader you bring unique expertise to one or another of Bob Roberts's domains. Your minister can't possibly know what it's like to be a Christian lawyer in a large legal practice or a scientific researcher in a multinational pharmaceutical company. He or she can help you to understand biblical theology—an essential part of the process—but you must become the expert, along with other Christians who share the same life and work experience. The goal is not only to ask how I must behave morally or ethically, or how I might share the gospel with my colleagues, or how I might be a good example of the values of Christ. It also includes questions about how I might shape my legal practice or my pharmaceutical company to operate more in line with the values of God's kingdom.

Excarnate impulses, however, have pulled Christians out of the domains of society and effectively created a ninth domain—the church. If we think of Roberts's domains as silos and add the church into the equation, they would be look something like figure 10.1.

| Economics | Agriculture | Education | Science/Tech | Communication | Arts | Politics/Law | Family | Church |
|---|---|---|---|---|---|---|---|---|
| | | | | | | | | |

**Figure 10.1. Nine silos (or domains) of society**

The Christian community does all it can do to bolster and strengthen that ninth silo, the church. Church leaders regularly claim that we need more and better churches to change the culture of the West, but what is the evidence for this? I recently attended a church planting conference where a video presentation was screened that detailed a litany of indications of the breakdown in American society—rates of divorce, crime, teen pregnancy, abortion, domestic violence and on and on. It was a deeply sobering look at the shape America is in. Then the film concluded with a call for us to plant more churches. Now, I'm not opposed to planting more and better churches, but where is the evidence that more churches leads to a better education sector or a better legal system or a better set of values for society in general? Surely, what America needs is not only more Christians, but more Christians who seek illumination from the gospel for daily life. Instead, we are seeing Christians leave the public school sector to teach in Christian schools. We are seeing churches establish film and music schools so Christian artists can create "Christian art" for use in churches. We have assumed that if we make the ninth silo stronger, it will affect the rest, but I fear it doesn't. We need capable Christian leaders in industry, education, the health sector and agriculture who are pursuing what the reign of God looks like in their field and actively seeking to effect change in their domain. Instead of seeing our mission as increasing the size and effectiveness of the church (see fig. 10.2),

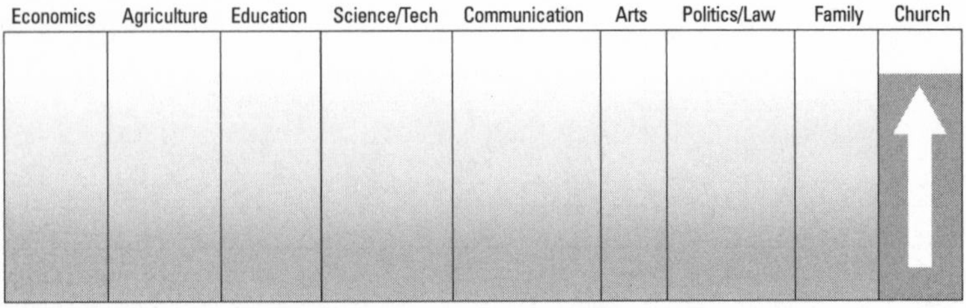

| Economics | Agriculture | Education | Science/Tech | Communication | Arts | Politics/Law | Family | Church |
|---|---|---|---|---|---|---|---|---|

Figure 10.2. Mission: Increase the size and effectiveness of the church

what if we looked at the church's mission as empowering followers of Christ to infiltrate all the domains of society as agents of the mission of God (see fig. 10.3)?[10]

Indeed, what if the church saw itself called to the brokering of meaningful consultations between committed Christian leaders in all eight of Roberts's domains with a view to exploring and promoting the demonstration of the universal reign of God in each of those domains?

This can be applied to a crosscultural setting as well. What if overseas missionaries influenced key Christian leaders in every domain? What if, instead of just clicking on online petitions opposing sex trafficking, we saw it as our role to move into Southeast Asia or Central and Eastern Europe with a view to equipping

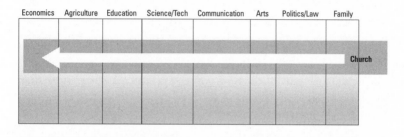

**Figure 10.3. Mission: Infiltrate all the domains of society as agents of the mission of God**

Christian law enforcement officers, judges, politicians and social workers to slowly but surely contribute to a shift in those cultures to make sex trafficking more difficult and less likely?

### EXCARNATIONAL EVANGELISM

Of course, the mission of God's people includes an *announcement* of that reign, not only its demonstration. I am ever mindful of David Bosch's words, "This message is indeed necessary. . . . It cannot be replaced by unexplained deeds."[11] In *The Road to Missional* I explore my vision for a missional approach to evangelism, one that involves more than simply giving people information about how to go to heaven when they die. Rather, evangelism is the announcement of the good news that Jesus is King, that he is putting everything under his peaceable and just reign, and calls on all peoples everywhere to acknowledge his rule and submit to it. Clearly, there's more to this than collaring someone on a street corner and asking them to pray the sinner's prayer. Indeed, I believe that the reliance on overly simple creeds like the sinner's prayer is another expression of excarnation. It expects that the outcome of successful evangelism is a transaction that takes place between the sinner and God entirely in the sinner's mind.

We must get back to the idea that people need to be evangelized in *bodily ways* as well as by the transfer of certain knowledge. This was the way of the rabbinic tradition. Acolytes sat at the feet of their rabbi and were instructed not only with ideas but with practices, liturgies and new experiences. Earlier, we looked at Michael Polanyi's idea of elbow learning, using Stradivari as an example. By sitting at the elbow of the master the apprentice learned more than anything he or she could have read in a manual. This can be applied to Christian discipleship, but I would suggest it is also a reasonable model for practicing embodied evangelism. After all, we see this in the way Jesus "evangelized" his disciples. I've heard Alan Hirsch ask conference delegates to identify the point at which Jesus' disciples became Christians. Was it when they accepted the call to follow him? Or when they came to understand his messianic identity? Or when they witnessed the resurrection? Or received the Holy Spirit? Or acknowledged the gospel was for the Gentiles? At every level their faith in Jesus deepens, and in every instance it is accompanied by embodied action. Why do we assume it's different for people becoming followers of Jesus today? Can one sermon and one prayer ever do the trick? Or is evangelism in an excarnate age necessarily going to include apprenticeship, enacted experience, ritual, pilgrimage and more?

Since, by even the most conservative definition, effective evangelism must result in transformation—repentance, acceptance, discipleship—then it makes sense to think through how humans are transformed. In *Practicing the Way of Jesus*, Mark Scandrette explores the dynamics of human transformation. He suggests eight dynamics need to be borne in mind when determining a process of change for someone.[12] While Scandrette doesn't directly relate this to evangelism, I think these dynamics can be applied here nonetheless. They are as follows.

1. *Transformation happens through new vision.* There's no question that a new vision, beliefs and perspectives have to be introduced for genuine change to take place. Therefore, evangelism necessarily must include the sharing of new ideas about the reign of King Jesus, ideas potential new believers could not work out by themselves.

2. *Transformation happens through new experiences.* New ideas are essential, but action brings true understanding of the reign of God through Christ. As Scandrette says, "When we risk going new places, meeting new people and risking new activities the resulting disequilibrium can create space for change."[13] That's because these new experiences shake our assumptions and prejudices, and create cracks in which the new truth of Jesus can take root. Effective evangelism must include a taste-and-see dimension as well as a listen-and-learn approach. This was the disciples' experience as described by the apostle John: "That . . . which we have heard, which we have seen with our eyes, which we have looked at and our hands have touched—this we proclaim concerning the Word of life" (1 John 1:1).

3. *Transformation happens through establishing new patterns of thought and action.* Scandrette points out that human beings are essentially creatures of instinct and habit, and that genuine transformation has to include replacing old habits with new patterns of life. We explored something similar in chapter seven when we looked at James K. A. Smith's insights into the habits that are formed in us by society and the need to foster alternative habits, liturgies and practices to sustain rightly ordered loves. Teaching people new habits as part of the evangelistic enterprise is equally important.

4. *Transformation happens through group encounter and reflection.* "We are much more likely to take steps to change in solidarity with others," says Scandrette.[14] In days gone by people embraced the Christian faith through the initiation rites of catechism and baptism

preparation. More recently, in the United Kingdom, Alpha has been the most widespread and effective evangelistic tool in use. It is a group activity that involves people eating a meal each week and exploring the meaning of the gospel. I acknowledge that many people want to sit at home and Google the answers to the questions they might have about Christianity, but I believe that whatever faith can emerge from finding answers at Wikipedia is an excarnate version, and we are right to insist on group encounter and reflection as an essential aspect of missional evangelism. Consider Alcoholics Anonymous and other Twelve-Step programs. It is the most effective transformational device in the world, and it insists on hospitable, gracious group solidarity.

5. *Transformation happens through good examples and guidance.* For the disciples this was Jesus. For participants in AA it is the leaders and their sponsors. Like the rabbinic tradition, those seeking to follow Jesus need guides, mentors and evangelistic spiritual directors to move them forward in their faith.

6. *Transformation happens through failures, setbacks, mistakes and persistence.* Excarnate evangelism expects converts to say a prayer, attend church and read their Bible every day. And should they fall back into old, unhelpful patterns of living that are incongruous with the gospel, they are readily expelled. But how many times did the disciples stumble or even abandon Jesus in their early journey of faith? New believers, and those still journeying toward faith, need to be offered not only a new vision of the world as Christ intends it, but new habits that bolster that vision, and a community of generous fellow travelers and mentors around them that allow them to fail and learn and move forward. Indeed, we learn and grow as much from our failures as our successes.

7. *Transformation into the likeness of Christ happens by the power of the Spirit.* Scandrette very helpfully shatters the dichotomy between intentional practices and public actions on the one hand and

the work of the Spirit on the other. We are to practice Jesus' teachings *and* rely on the power of leading of the Holy Spirit. They are not mutually exclusive areas. He says, "The Spirit is at work any time transformation into Christlikeness takes place. We are invited to do whatever we can to surrender to the work of the Spirit in us, and pray and expect God's kindness to also lead others toward transformation."[15]

*8. Transformation is rooted in the heart.* This is Mark's way of cautioning us not to entirely externalize our faith and assume practices and actions alone constitute the sum of following Christ. He concludes powerfully,

> A group practice doesn't guarantee a change of heart for anyone, but it does create a supportive environment where transformation is likely to occur. [Group projects] can expose where heart renovation is needed. Real substantive change occurs as we learn to surrender to the will and authority of the Creator from the core of who we are. A change of heart can begin inwardly or outwardly, but always involves surrendering to the will and power of God.[16]

## WHY BOTHER LEAVING THE HOUSE?

Charles Finney (1792-1875) has been called the father of American revivalism. He was the first to popularize the "protracted meeting" and the first to employ the use of the "anxious bench" for those under conviction of sin, later known as "the altar call." He also strongly influenced evangelist Dwight L. Moody, who followed similar measures. It is regularly claimed that they were the architects of the approach to evangelism that fostered highly individualized and internalized "decisions for Christ." And yet Finney was a fiery abolitionist, and both men were advocates of women's suffrage and equal opportunity for education. It is said that Moody, after he had called people to come forward to follow Jesus, immediately instructed them then to proceed to the back of the hall and sign up to the local temperance league and women's suffrage movement. He is also credited with launching the Student Volunteer Movement that saw tens of thousands of young men and women head overseas to serve God as missionaries. To them the gospel had corporate, global and political implications as well as personal ones.

Today it is assumed that is it possible to serve God without ever even leaving your house or the church. We can engage in global issues via the Internet. We can be kept safe from the sullying influences of the world "out there." And we can run evangelism campaigns that ask strangers to come into our churches, make decisions and never be seen again. We can listen to our favorite preachers via their podcasts and play our most beloved worship songs as MP3s. But I contend none of that will change us and very little of that will result in lasting transformation in our communities either. We need to get out of the house. We need to move into the neighborhood and rub shoulders with those who don't yet share our faith. We need to develop joint practices or habits with like-minded followers of Jesus that bind us more deeply to God, to each other, and which propel us outward into the lives of others, especially the poor, the lost and the lonely.

Ben Saunders is a modern-day polar explorer in the same fashion as Ernest Shackleton or Robert Peary. He has successfully walked across the ice from one side of the arctic circle to the other, and at the time of writing this book was attempting to be the first man to walk from the Ross Sea ice shelf in Antarctica to the South Pole and back, a feat never before completed, even by Robert Falcon Scott, who died during the attempt in 1912. Recently, as part of the TED series of short talks, he attempted to answer the question why we should even bother to attempt such feats. After all, doesn't the constant supply of information about every corner of the world affect our motivation for going to such challenging places? If it is being done somewhere by someone, and we can participate in it virtually, then why bother leaving the house? In part, this was his answer:

> Our lives are safer and more comfortable than they have ever been. . . . If I wanted to know, for example, how many stars were in the Milky Way or how old those giant heads on Easter Island were, most of you could find that out now without even standing up. And yet if I've learnt anything from nearly twelve years now of dragging heavy things around cold places, it is that true, real, inspiration and growth only comes from adversity and from challenge, from stepping away from what's comfortable and familiar and stepping out into the unknown.[17]

Amen!

# 11

## Placed Persons

*If we are not spiritual where we are and as we are,*
*we are not spiritual at all.*

JOAN CHICHESTER

🔳

Once, after a hectic speaking schedule in Phnom Penh, Cambodia, I happened to have the day off alone on my birthday. At first I didn't mind that idea. I thought I'd sleep in a little longer than usual, take a leisurely breakfast by the pool in my cheap hotel, wander down the street to the city's famous Central Market to buy a gift for my wife, and then meander carelessly around the teeming streets, taking in the sights and sounds of this fascinating city. Wrong. Sleeping in and breakfasting by the pool worked out, but everything else was a disaster. You see, Phnom Penh is not a city for pedestrians. Not only are the roads clogged with bikes, trucks and cars, the sidewalks are littered with hawkers, food carts and motorbikes. In fact, the sidewalks themselves are cracked and broken due to the excessive use of cars and bikes illegally parking on them. Walking through Phnom Penh in the heat of the day, trying to avoid tripping or being run down or knocked over requires maximum attention. Strolling, meandering or wandering was out of the question. Just getting to and from the Central Market was an exhausting enterprise, not to mention how overwhelming it was to be harassed and bustled by the stallholders, all pressing me to buy their wares. Even before lunch, I had stumbled back to my tiny air-conditioned hotel room defeated by the city. I tried again that afternoon, hoping to get down to the banks of the Tonlé Sap River for a stroll along the promenade, but I was driven back by the bustle and the heat. I ended up spending a depressing day in my dingy hotel room on my birthday.

In Phnom Penh the motorbike is everything. Without one you're trapped in a very small part of your environment. In this way, the built environment shapes the residents' sense of community and well-being. But is it much different in American cities? Well, it looks very different at first glance, but it isn't much different in reality. I was once the guest of some friends of a friend in Thousand Oaks, in the northwestern part of Greater Los Angeles. Thousand Oaks has been named one of the "best places to live" by some investment magazine or other. Situated in the Conejo Valley in Ventura County, and featuring, you guessed it, an abundance of Californian oak trees, it is a typical American suburban community with well-manicured lawns and neat houses arranged in cul-de-sacs. I once spent a free day in this city as well, and surprisingly I had a very similar experience to my birthday in Phnom Penh.

Initially I thought I would stroll to the downtown area and get some lunch and take in the sights, but my hosts informed me that Thousand Oaks has no downtown. It was part of a master-planned city created by the Janss Investment Company in the mid-1950s, which included about three thousand dwellings built around the Janss Marketplace shopping mall. Since then several other malls and many other residences have popped up. Okay, I conceded, I'll walk down to the mall then. No, I was informed, that would be impossible. For a start, none of the streets in the area where I was staying has sidewalks, and second, to get to the mall from the house required crossing a freeway, which was impossible on foot. Indeed, if the neighbors saw a strange man wandering the empty streets of their community, it would arouse some suspicion. My hosts were heading out to work for the day, taking both the cars, so I was effectively trapped in the house. It was a very comfortable house, and my hosts were very generous, but in reality I was as stuck in their palatial house as I was in that cheap hotel in Phnom Penh. In both cases I resorted to the Internet to check email and social media.

Our cities seem to be designed, for different reasons, to keep us excarnate. This was the very thing Jane Jacobs was alerting us to a generation ago when she rather colorfully described what housing developers have given us. They are

> low income projects that become worse centers of delinquency, vandalism and general social hopelessness than the slums they were supposed to replace; middle income housing projects which are truly marvels of dullness and regimentation, sealed against any buoyancy or vitality of city life; luxury housing projects that mitigate their inanity with a vapid vulgarity; cultural centers that are unable to support a good bookstore; civic centers that are avoided by everyone but bums, who have fewer choices of loitering than others; commercial centers that are lacklustre imitations of standardized suburban chain store shopping; promenades that go from no place to nowhere and have no promenaders; expressways that eviscerate great cities. This is not the rebuilding of cities, *this is the sacking of cities*.[1]

Of course, housing developments and city planning are driven entirely by commercial interests. Their "sacking of the city" is to their gain. So indeed was the development of the Internet, as James Hunter alerted us. Those who make decisions about both our built environment and our electronic environment are not interested in community, justice, amenity or just plain neighborliness. They're just trying to make a buck. And as a result we live in neighborhoods that are simply unwalkable. We allow builders to create houses with façades that look like fortresses, with all the family life tucked away in the rear and surrounded by walls so high that no one can see in. We live, glued to our screens, playing games, checking social media, interacting in the flattened, fragmented world of the Internet. We have happily acquiesced to the architects of modern secular living and allowed them to shape our environment according to whatever will make them the biggest return. And none of these planners or builders will ever have to live with the consequences of the cities and neighborhoods they create. As theologian Jürgen Moltmann concludes, "Predatory exploitation is practised only by alien and homeless groups of people."[2] Interestingly, the protected lives of those who live in gated communities and walled houses might be pleasant enough, but it is inhumane due to the lack of human closeness and community, while the unprotected life of the slums has far greater potential for a truly humane community. Living in a poor urban neighborhood might bring certain dangers, but raising children in a suburban estate brings its own dangers. It's just that we don't rate being raised as a self-centered, egotistic consumer as all that dangerous.

### GLOBAL POSITIONING SYSTEMS AND THE EARTH

If the Internet and urban and suburban community planning play their part in our excarnation from place, so do other forms of technology, like the car and the humble GPS. In fact, I want to raise questions about what the GPS has done to our sense of place by eliminating the need for local knowledge and spatial awareness.

My wife is spatially challenged, to say the least. Getting lost was an art form for her, and one she exercised as regularly as possible.

It meant she was forever pulling over to read maps (usually upside down or sideways), approaching strangers for directions and generally visiting parts of the city she would never have otherwise visited. Then along came global positioning systems technology, first in specially designed devices for her vehicle and then, even more conveniently, in her phone. She has been set free. It has been a remarkably empowering new form of technology for her, allowing her greater autonomy and saving her great embarrassment. So, I'm not dismissing helpfulness or the importance of your humble GPS.

I like to think I have a pretty good sense of direction. I travel a lot and am fairly adept at working out my east from my west, or the coast from the mountain range, or the river from the plains. Having acclimatized myself to the direction the sun sets and putting the river or the coast or the mountains on my left or right, I'm generally pretty good at finding my way around. Well, in a general sense, at least. But the GPS supersedes all that. There's no need to worry about major landforms any longer. Put an address in your phone and the inbuilt GPS does the rest.

Our connection to the places we visit, or even the places we live in, is being eroded by technology. It began with the car. Once we no longer walked our neighborhoods or cities, gliding through or *over* them in motor vehicles, we lost something of our embodied sense of place. Now, thanks to the GPS, we don't even have to remain mindful of our surroundings. I have a friend who is as equally spatially challenged as my wife. He often jokes that he can't wait until GPS technology can be hardwired into our brains. Now, while I'm not dismissing the freedom that such technology can afford those who would otherwise find themselves hopelessly lost in new surroundings, I do want to question what we would lose if, to use my friend's fanciful idea, the GPS could be hardwired into our brains.

Negotiating your way through a new city or neighborhood takes *attentiveness*. We must pay attention to landforms, the direction of the sun in the sky and the built environment. And when we do lose our way without a GPS, we are forced to throw ourselves on the good graces of strangers or neighbors and ask for directions. Furthermore, consider the difference in our appreciation of a place when we are forced to get out of our motor vehicles and walk. All these forces have combined to create a loss of the experience of being rooted in a place, to really know our neighbors, to truly belong to the community, to feel deeply and responsibly that there is a bond between ourselves and the land, ourselves and the neighborhood, that nourishes and replenishes our beings.

## COMMUNITY IN THE BUILT ENVIRONMENT

In the face of this relentless excarnation, or *dis*-placement, Tim Gorringe, in *A Theology of the Built Environment*, explores six dimensions of the church to which we must ever hold fast.[3] Indeed, as we embrace these six dimensions, we provide hope to our defleshed, displaced world that there is another way that human beings can live together. Much like the Japanese gardens in the Honolulu airport I mentioned in chapter one, we can be the rich verdant alternative to liminal gate lounge experience of many secular people. Let's explore these six dimensions

First, the church is a *local* community, globally networked. In the face of what has been called the "shapeless giantism" of the great cities, people are yearning for and discovering the value and necessity of the neighborhood. The kids of the baby boom generation, who gave us Thousand Oaks, want a greater sense of place, community, neighborliness. Interestingly, Gorringe points out that as long ago as the 1930s American town planner Clarence Perry was recommending that a neighborhood should be "small enough for everything to be within walking distance, but large enough to support an elementary school, local stores and services."[4] In their book *Greening the Built Environment*, the authors recommend a neighborhood should have "streets laid out on rectangular grids to provide maximum connectivity, and the slowing down of traffic to enable people of diverse backgrounds to meet frequently, informally and for different purposes."[5] Compare this to the current preference for cul-de-sacs, major thoroughfares and freeways. Today, people live in one neighborhood, work in another and play in yet another. However, it is also true that the micropolitics of education, health, transport and even street design remains obstinately local. And as Gorringe points out, the importance of the local remains especially obvious for children, the elderly and the disabled. Churches must take this challenge seriously and see themselves as a localizing agency within a neighborhood, throwing their halls open for community use, funding local initiatives and enterprises, supporting local businesses, praying for their neighbors, and indeed introducing neighbors to each other. The opportunities for the church to be like salt and light in this respect are considerable.

Second, the church lives by *memory and tradition*. At a time when church tradition is being dismissed by everyone, including the church itself, Gorringe makes the valuable point that in many communities the church offers us the deepest roots. He refers to the cathedral cities in the United Kingdom and the way the churches in those places anchor communities in a shared belief system, a common history and set of values. This hardly relates to suburban neighborhoods in the United States, but it is nonetheless usually true that often the local church in suburban neighborhoods is the most permanent thing in town. Where businesses come and go, very few other agencies stick it out through thick and thin. The church is one. Sometimes, we look at a small church comprising mainly elderly folks and wonder what impact such a group could have. But it is helpful to think that this community of faith forms a repository of old wisdom, memory and long-term shared practice. These are extremely valuable resources in a time of excarnation, if only the church could figure out how to share them with their neighbors.

I think it was Simone Weil who said that humans don't survive without roots, and I believe she is right. Sociologists claim that long-time residents make a disproportionally large contribution to a community. But compare this to the highly mobile society in which many of us live. Apparently, the average American lives in one place for five years, a statistic that applies to Christians and the clergy as much as to anyone. I believe Christians should be the most rooted people in their community; their loyalty and devotion to a particular geographical area and everyone who lives there should be legendary. I live in the neighborhood where I grew up. I have deep, long-term connections with the place and with the community. I went to school with the head of the Chamber of Commerce. I share in the history of our village, knowing what problems it has overcome (ocean pollution, high-rise development) and what vexing struggles it avoids addressing (affordable housing, alcohol-related crime). And I drastically limit the amount of travel I do to ensure that my primary energy goes into the local.

It's not only our shared memory that the church can foster in a neighborhood, it is as the repository of local traditions that we can come into our own. If you've ever been in Britain or Europe over Christmastime, you will have seen the enormous effect of local Christmas markets that bring the whole community together around tradition, food and festivity. In the grounds around churches and in the squares beyond, decorations and gifts are sold, gluhwein (mulled wine) is served, pastries and pretzels are eaten, and parents supervise their children on carnival rides. In a very obvious sense, the church brings the town together at that time of year.

Third, the church is a community where *sin is recognized and forgiveness asked for*. In an interesting take on the church's contribution to community, Gorringe argues that we have much to offer if we rediscover our central tenets of confession, repentance and forgiveness. When practiced well, they foster a faith community of acceptance, hospitality and grace, a community that fights graciously, acknowledges all and is nourished by every contribution. Gorringe says, "A community which lives by sin and forgiveness is not a community of consensus, but a community which has found a way of coping with conflict and difference."[6] In an age when sociologists are crying out for ways for communities to practice tolerance, acceptance and grace, the church ought to be a microcosm of these very things. Indeed, surely the only way for these values to be inculcated in a neighborhood is for face-to-face negotiation to take place, and no agency in society seems ready or prepared to broker such discussions. Why not the church? Gorringe again:

> The task of the church in plural societies is to both support and radically criticize the framework which holds a plural society together, but also to be an active protagonist for minority-group positions. . . . Without this, community degenerates into communalism, in which community is pitted against community.[7]

How often have you heard stories of churches in conflict with their neighbors or with city hall? How often has the church degenerated into communalism and contributed to social breakdown rather than offering themselves as brokers in the development of better cities? Churches should take social issues head-on. We should practice peacemaking and offer our services to the neighborhood. We should be the "experts" on confession and forgiveness, teaching our community a better way forward, aiding our neighbors to become more tolerant, hospitable and welcoming. At a time when our cities are calling for greater tolerance toward others, the church can show what moving beyond mere tolerance looks like. *Tolerance* is one of the watchwords of a liberal society, but it is essentially passive. Christians understand that the proper response to the stranger is more proactive—it is expressed in the biblical practice of hospitality. Tolerance is the response of the powerful to the less powerful. It carries no imperative to actively help those who are vulnerable, whereas hospitality calls us to enter into relationship with those who are different.

Fourth, *justice* is essential to community. It seems patently wrong that some of the residents in our cities live in slums or bleak housing estates while others live in mansions in gated communities. The church's contribution to the place it finds itself is to contribute continually to this ideal, holding the city to its belief in the equal treatment of equals, and offering practical assistance to those left behind in the rush toward wealth creation. As the former archbishop of Canterbury Rowan Williams says,

> The Church exists to connect people at the level of their hunger for a new world. . . . [T]his is how the Church makes neighbors—not so much by struggling to find ideas that unite us, not even by struggling to make us like each other, but by giving us a role to play, the role of people all equally eager to be fed by one life-giving food.[8]

I cannot help but recall the recent courage of the Church of Scotland minister in a housing estate near Glasgow, Scotland, who confronted local hatreds by throwing open his church day and night as a safe space for Muslim refugees when one of them was assaulted and murdered.

Fifth, the church is committed to a *common purpose*, their shared final ends. The universal church is called together by a common story and bound together by a common hope. In this respect, we are indeed a "purpose-driven" people (with apologies to Rick Warren). In being formed distinctly and uniquely by our shared hope in the future promised by God, we know how to be resolutely future oriented. The Spirit of God is calling us on this journey both as pilgrims (we are shaped by a narrative of where we are going and a sense of how to go on that journey) but also as wayfarers (we're leaving a place that has been familiar, where we mastered the practices of being church but now travel in terra incognito with a sense of loss and disorientation). The way for such pilgrims/wayfarers is a journey of mutuality and respect among strangers in our local communities without predetermined solutions or formulas; we will need to experiment and discern. This, says Gorringe, is a skill sorely needed by our broader communities. He quotes Kevin Lynch's 1960 book, *The Image of City*, saying that the city landscape should express the common hopes and pleasures of ordinary people, so that "the sense of community may be made flesh."[9] Lynch continued, "Above all, if the environment is visibly organized and sharply identified, then it will become a *place*, remarkable and unmistakable."[10] In other words, in order for the city to survive as a viable public space, it must be able to articulate its genuinely common hopes and pleasures. And who will broker the negotiation of what those hopes and pleasures are? Why couldn't it be the church?

As it happens, in my city it was the trade union movement that brokered an alliance of concerned residents to discuss ways to foster a more socially just, safe and compassionate place. Called the Sydney Alliance, their stated goal was to bring together diverse community organizations, unions and religious organizations to advance the common good and achieve a fair, just and sustainable city. Their website says, "We do this by providing opportunities for people to have a say in decisions that affect them, their families and everyone working and living in Sydney."[11] Admittedly, some churches have agreed to participate, but it's disappointing that churches aren't at the forefront of catalyzing such conversations around the world. Gorringe says, "To the objection that this is too abstract a thing for people to commit themselves to, the answer is that what we are talking about is the sharing and safeguarding of the basic resources of life, and there is nothing more concrete than this."[12]

Sixth, the church is *semper reformanda*, always in the process of re-creation and rediscovery. Having earlier reminded us of the value of memory and tradition, Gorringe also points out, "Though we are committed to the attempt to construct community, this will always be fragile, always in need of re-invention."[13] And so it should be, with each generation of Christ followers committed to new, fresh expressions of what our place could be like. It keeps us from maintaining some dull status quo, and from our fear of failure in our attempts at experimentation. In the United Kingdom there is a growing awareness of the role churches can play in urban renewal. The Church of England Commission on Urban Life and Faith recently reported on the way government perceives the contribution of religious communities to such regeneration:

> However, as far as the Government is concerned, religion (however sketchily that is perceived) still remains among the most significant elements of civil society and community mobilization. And, as a Commission, we have also heard time and again how shared service within local communities has given rise to opportunities for inter-faith dialogue and common purpose—and of the new opportunities these present for a united witness for the good of the city. These seem to us to focus around three themes:
> - The renewed commitment to regeneration and neighbourhood renewal that is coming from many quarters;
> - The intriguing use of language of human flourishing and spirituality in the hopes and visions for what makes a good city;
> - The challenge to celebrate and support the many sources and expressions of faith which are taking place in the city.[14]

# 12

# Adopting an Incarnational Posture

*Until we too have taken the idea of the God-man seriously*
*enough to be scandalized by it, we have not taken it*
*as seriously as it demands to be taken.*

FREDERICK BUECHNER

n 2011, journalist Nicholas Carr noticed he was having trouble focusing. When he sat down to read a book he could barely get through a page without his mind wandering off on a tangent. He also had trouble focusing on other tasks and couldn't remember things as well as he used to. It began to occur to him that his use of the Internet might have been to blame. His book *The Shallows: What the Internet Is Doing to Our Brains* was the result of his research into his own loss of concentration and attention. His book describes in detail, with lots of scientific facts about brain activity, why we're finding ourselves so distracted nowadays. In essence, his thesis is that significant use of new media changes the way our brain works, including reducing our ability to focus.

This got me thinking about other kinds of new technology. It might well be that Google is making us stupid (to steal the title of an earlier article by Carr), but what about excessive reliance on GPS technology? Could that actually make us even more lost than we were before? Carr is on to this hypothesis as well. He describes how all kinds of new technologies make us lose part of ourselves. Clocks made us lose our natural rhythm and maps made us lose our spatial recognition capacities. Neil Postman pointed out as much in his book *Amusing Ourselves to Death*, when he said that the introduction of the telegraph meant the loss of the sense of the local, because news from all over trumped news associated with local events and happenings. Technology collapsed of the idea of geography and distance. But Nicholas Carr reserves his most scathing critique for the Internet, claiming that unlike most other technologies, it is making us lose our touch with the real world. Our brains jump around constantly as if we are browsing websites. We feel pressured to be always looking at our phones and computers and replying to messages. The end result is that we live more and more inside the Internet, and when we need to leave it, we can't work as well as we previously could. Sounds excarnate, doesn't it? Carr writes,

> A series of psychological studies over the past twenty years has revealed that after spending time in a quiet rural setting, close to nature, people exhibit greater attentiveness, stronger memory, and generally improved cognition. Their brains become both calmer and sharper. The reason, according to attention restoration theory, or ART, is that when people aren't being bombarded by external stimuli, their brains can, in effect, relax.[1]

How fascinating that science is telling us to get off the Internet and live in a more embodied way in a place that allows us to connect to nature and community. Sadly, too many of Carr's readers will over-react and take this mean that we have to join an Amish community in Pennsylvania or Ontario to get our brains working properly again. I think there is a way to embody our faith in place without moving to a barn in Lancaster County. But first we need to come to terms with the ways excarnation is changing our sense of well-being and our connection to place. In an interview, French philosopher Paul Virilio said,

> We now have the possibility of seeing at a distance, of hearing at a distance, and of acting at a distance, and this results in a process of de-localization, of the unrooting of the being. "To be" used to mean to be somewhere, to be situated, in the here and now, but the "situation" of the essence of being is undermined by the instantaneity, the immediacy, and the ubiquity which are characteristic of our epoch. Our contemporaries will henceforth need two watches: one to watch the time, the other to watch the place where one actually is.[2]

Never knowing where one really is, is one of the great dilemmas of our time. This unrooting of the human experience into some perpetual *no place* only reinforces the process of excarnation. James Hunter, in his book *To Change the World*, discusses the impact of technology on our ability to access information, and particularly on the way it is reshaping intimacy between persons and their connection to geographical place. He claims that the emergence of electronic media has transformed the nature of human consciousness and culture as well, suggesting four broad effects:

1. The Internet transforms time and space by radically "compressing them," meaning that "time is shortened and space is shrunken to the point where they almost disappear."[3] In other words, people halfway around the globe feel as present as if they were in the next room, thus eliminating any sense of geography or place.

2. Electronic media seamlessly, rapidly and intensely compartmentalize the world and put its parts together in incoherent

ways with no overarching narrative structure. "The fictional and the real, the comical and the serious, the insignificant and the significant, all blend together flattening out the distinctions among them. The net effect is that all content is trivialized."[4]

Driven as they are by commercial interests, radio, television and the Internet presents information chiefly through the format of entertainment. This was Neil Postman's chief concern in *Amusing Ourselves to Death*. Information as entertainment naturally contributes to the trivialization of meaningful content. As Hunter says, "Since the goal is to generate positive approval from as large an audience as possible, content has to be driven by the audience's changing wishes and inclinations."[5]

3. Finally, these media "create an illusion of intimacy with actors, politicians, talk show hosts, sports celebrities, and strangers with whom we do business because we share the same conversational space."[6] As a result, all information that is obviously public in nature is received as deeply private as well, blurring the distinction between the political and the personal, the important and the trivial.

All this becomes increasingly concerning when we consider that fact that human consciousness is never independent of the social circumstances in which it is lived. Our view of the world never transcends the world it is embedded in. So if our worldview is composed of merely surface images and simulations, fragmented and flattened in the way Hunter describes, little wonder people find it difficult to embrace meaningful reflection, deep relationships, lifelong commitments or an abiding sense of connection to place. As Hunter says,

It is difficult to discover the quality of intimacy in a friendship or in love that is nurtured through time and attentiveness to the subtleties of need, memory, joy, and hurt. So too, it is difficult to forge moral commitments capable of enduring the vagaries of hardship, boredom, failure.[7]

More so, it forces us to consider what on earth the Christian message can say into such a world, where it is difficult to imagine that there is a spiritual reality more real than the material world we live in. Hunter sums it up,

> Altogether these media foster a reality that exists primarily if not only within the surfaces of sensory awareness and understanding. This is a world constituted by image, representation, simulation, and illusion. This is, of course, a highly engineered reality that distances us from our natural surroundings and the immediacy of primary relationships. It is a simulated reality that, in many ways, supersedes lived reality.[8]

"Lived reality" is a local, embedded relational experience. In the simulated world, place, geography, the built environment, history, memory and shared experience all take on different—I would say, *reduced*—value. It is not only the emergence of new media that is to blame. The kinds of cities we build contribute dramatically to the defleshing of our sense of place.

Bearing all this in mind, what are the implications of this for Christians wishing to countermand the excarnational impulses that pull us up and out of our neighborhoods? How can we go down and deep into the cities and villages where God has placed us? Let's think of Gorringe's six dimensions in terms of innovation. How can we adopt the posture, thinking, behavior and practices of an incarnational one to engage our communities meaningfully and for God's glory? I'd like to make four simple suggestions:

1. *Anthropologically (move in).* What can we do to become more embedded in our communities, to appreciate their needs, hopes

and yearnings? Moving into the neighborhood is essential. Can you imagine marrying your spouse, then choosing to live separately? It is so common a thing these days for Christians to attend churches several neighborhoods away that raising the question seems strangely redundant. But I continue to raise it. What sense does it make for all the Christians in America to be getting into gas-guzzling SUVs every Sunday morning and crisscrossing their greater metro regions to go to a church in some distant community? Compare this with a recent article titled "Most Americans Want a Walkable Neighborhood, Not a Big House," which highlights the changing mentality of Americans. It says, "Six in 10 people also said they would sacrifice a bigger house to live in a neighborhood that featured a mix of houses, stores, and businesses within an easy walk."[9] Why wouldn't the church want to lead the way in modeling what this could look like?

It's heartening to hear of the Walkable Church movement, a network of church leaders who are trying to promote walkability as a core church value. One of its proponents, Sean Benesh, leads a church in Portland called the Ion Community. He says, "Out of the 5 core values that identifies the Ion Community, one of them is related solely to transportation. I believe that if there is one value that could potentially set the Ion Community apart from many churches it is this value: Walkable."[10] Being able to walk to church isn't some magical missional practice, but it does ensure that con-gregations will be an enfleshed presence in their immediate com-munity. At the very least, pastors should aim to live and serve in the same neighborhood where their church is. I am often surprised to hear church leaders ask me whether it matters where they live. But what did Jesus do? He was called Immanuel ("God with us"), and he chose to make "his home among us." We mirror his character in this world when we move in and embrace solidarity with the place where God has sent us. Kathleen Norris writes, "To be an

American is to move on, as if we could outrun change. To attach oneself to place is to surrender to it, and suffer with it."[11]

2. *Empathically (listen to them)*. René Laennec, the inventor of the stethoscope, famously said, "Listen to your patients, they are telling you how to heal them." In *A Secular Age*, Charles Taylor questions what occurred between 1500 and 2000—the modern age of Western society—when in 2000 it was possible not to believe in God, while in 1500 it was impossible to do so. His answer: disenchantment, which led to secularism. According to Taylor, disenchantment "leaves us with a universe that is dull, routine, flat, driven by rules rather than thoughts, a process that culminates in bureaucracy run by specialists without spirit, hedonists without heart."[12] This is the world our community lives in. The church must adopt a posture of active listening, of attentiveness to the disenchantment of our neighbors, in order to know how to offer something more than the deathly, heartless, hedonistic world of secularism.

3. *Collaboratively (partner with them)*. Gorringe raises various ways that the church can collaborate with their neighbors: as the source of confession and forgiveness, as the repositories of memory and tradition, as the purveyors of justice and mercy, as the brokers of a new conversation about the future of the city. Who else is invested in meeting the needs of the community and committed to working together in a multidisciplinary manner to meet those needs? Churches sometimes defraud their mission of alerting others to the universal reign of God for the sake of building their own kingdom. Just like any entrepreneur, they can be overly concerned with some return on their investment. But if we truly take a kingdom approach to restoring our cities, we should be willing to partner with other churches, businesses, city officials and social organizations to meet the needs of the city. For example, on Magnolia Avenue in Fort Worth, Texas, you'll find an extremely cool coffee house, pub and eatery called *Brewed*, serving specialty craft bev-

erages alongside a very tasty menu. It was the brainchild of local missionary Joey Turner, who specifically located it in a rundown section of Magnolia in order to bring regeneration to the neighborhood. In fact, he not only consulted city hall and the business community, but he asked a number of homeless men in the area which was the best boarded-up building to put it in. One of them now works as a janitor in the space. Joey's vision wasn't just to fashion a living room for the locals (although he's definitely done that!), but also to bring life back to a dead and dangerous part of town. And the people of Fort Worth love *Brewed* for its collaboration with their neighborhood.

4. *Sustainably (stay with them—for a long time).* The people who build our neighborhoods have no long-term interest in them. They are concerned chiefly with obtaining approvals so that they could build and sell their homes and leave town in a cloud of dust after they've closed out. Is it possible that church planters and other professional clergy can be seen the same way? Many of them are around for long enough to close out their deal (or vision, as they like to call it) before moving on to the next venture. Perception is reality, until we change it. Like a marriage, church leadership should be for the longest time, to be wedded to a community through thick and thin, come what may. As Wendell Berry points out, "Make a home. Help to make a community. Be loyal to what you have made. Put the interests of your community first. Love your neighbors—not the neighbors you pick out, but the ones you have."[13]

### Mission-in-Place as a Spiritual Practice

The Missional Network, headed by Alan Roxburgh, has been encouraging an ongoing discussion of the idea of mission in a particular place as a spiritual practice. The network began initially to answer a question posed by Lesslie Newbigin over thirty years ago: What is the nature of a missionary encounter with the late-modern culture that shapes the West? Their answers have led them to the following five convictions:

1. Because the missionary God is at work in the shifting, turbulent contexts of western societies—the churches are called to enter a new imagination for being God's people.

2. This requires disciples of Jesus to be shaped by disciplines and practices.

3. Local contexts are where God's ordinary people discern the activity of God.

4. The Spirit is leading us on a journey of mutuality and respect toward our neighborhoods and communities.

5. There are no preferred solutions or formulas. Experimentation and innovation are important gifts for this journey.[14]

On the basis of these convictions, Roxburgh then turned his attention to the idea of mission-in-place as a spiritual practice, or more accurately, a series of practices. What rhythms of life or habits will sustain us as we seek to live in embodied, incarnational ways in the communities where God has placed us? When we considers the usual life of the typical church, it is plain to see that it is inculcated shared practices among its members—weekly attendance at worship, daily prayer, group study of the Bible and so forth. Roxburgh's questions have to do with whether there are other, or even different, practices we would be better off promoting. He says,

> Such a re-imagining requires the church, first and foremost, to ask what it means to be re-socialized into a way of life that posits the gospel as an alternative narrative to that of late modernity. This is a prima facie requirement of a missionary encounter with our culture. How do we take this journey? What are the guides for this strange path on which God's Spirit is leading us?[15]

In answering his own question he turns to Jesus' commissioning of his disciples in Luke 10:1-12. This is an oft-quoted text in missional church circles, and at times I fear too much can be made of it. It is neither a magic formula, nor a blueprint for all Christian mission. I don't believe Jesus was establishing the *exact* shape of Christian mission for all the ages in Luke 10. Indeed, it is clear that the passage needs to be read in light of Luke 8—the parable of the sower— where Jesus explicitly states that in this phase of the kingdom of God the message must be broadcast far and wide, and as quickly as possible. Knowing that some seed will fall along the path, some on rocky ground, some among thorns and some on good soil, the imperative at this stage of his ministry seems to be to scatter the message as broadly as possible. This in turn makes sense of his instructions to his disciples in Luke 10 to wipe the dust from their feet and move on should a town or village not accept their message. Of course, this is the very opposite of what we've been discussing— a long-term commitment to the same people in the same place. Jesus' is conscious of his limited time. He must disseminate his message as widely as he can, so he instructs his disciples to leave unresponsive communities, something that has been used by itinerant evangelists to justify their translocal ministries for centuries. Let me say, I do believe some of us will be called to translocal work, but they are the exceptions who prove the rule.

Nonetheless, I agree with Roxburgh that the greater use of Luke 10 lies in the way it has set an alternative missional posture for the followers of Jesus, one that can be readily embraced even by those of us who choose to stay put in the neighborhoods he has given us. First, as Roxburgh says, it "re-orients the *focus* of the church's activities from within and among themselves into the communities where they dwell."[16] This is unmistakable in Luke 10. There is no prefabricated ministry, no prepared suite of missional products to be presented, no firm model of church. The commissioning in this passage sets the followers of Jesus on a decidedly outward-oriented trajectory. Second, Roxburgh says it "reframes the *location of the questions*" asked by the disciples themselves.[17] Rather than making ecclesiocentric inquiries, the disciples are forced to interrogate the situation differently. Their questions are theocentric. An ecclesiocentric question would be, How do we fix the church? Whereas a theocentric one is, How do we discern what God is doing ahead of us in our communities? This shifts the agenda from asking what *we* should do to an exploration of how we are to join with what *God* is already doing ahead of us in our communities. From there Roxburgh then distills a series of practices from the text. As I mentioned earlier, these should not be seen as a straightjacket or a fixed blueprint, but rather as a collection of habits that can be worked out differently in their unique situations.

The passage begins:

> After this the Lord appointed seventy-two others and sent them two by two ahead of him to every town and place where he was about to go. He told them, "The harvest is plentiful, but the workers are few. Ask the Lord of the harvest, therefore, to send out workers into his harvest field. Go! I am sending you out like lambs among wolves." (Luke 10:1-3)

What follows is a series of instructions, or to use Roxburgh's parlance, "a set of practices that shape their journey." They are

- *Operate in community.* The disciples are sent out in pairs, ensuring that their missional DNA is rooted in a social construction rather than individualism. I am not suggesting that, like Mormon missionaries, we should duplicate this exactly and start knocking on doors in pairs. Rather, I think it is important that as we seek to reembody our faith in context, we should be seen as serving alongside others. Join the PTA *with others*. Eat regularly in the same coffee shop *with others*. Make the assumption that the default setting for church practice is communal.

- *Collaborate with the neighborhood.* This point was made earlier, but I reiterate it here in light of Jesus' advice to his followers that they not take a purse or bag or sandals on their journey (v. 4). At the very least this would force them to become dependent on the hospitality of their host community, ensuring a mutual collaboration or partnership in their endeavors together.

- *Declare the shalom of God.* As Alan Roxburgh points out, this was not a polite, formal greeting. These disciples were walking where the Roman Empire had previously proposed their Pax Romana. If the residents of the towns they visited remained loyal to Rome, then they would be offered a measure of security. The message of the disciples was that shalom comes from God alone. It was a radical counternarrative to the imperial control of Caesar. An important spiritual practice today must be speaking an alternative story to the American dream or the promises of middle-class security.

- *Identify persons of peace.* Much has been written in recent times about the importance of the discovery of "persons of peace" in a host community. Alan Hirsch and I wrote about this in *The Shaping of Things to Come*, where we said, "People of peace are key people who are spiritually open, have good reputations, and have influence in the community."[18] In Luke 10 we see Jesus instructing his disciples to look for such people (v. 6). That is to say, those people who accept the radical declaration that the shalom of God trumps the specious claims of the Pax Romana are those with whom the disciples are to spend their time. Paul followed this approach in Corinth by focusing his efforts in the home of Priscilla and Aquila, the local tentmakers (Acts 18:1-4). Likewise, we need to move into the neighborhood, making radical declarations about the peace of God and see which influencers rise to the calling.

- *Enter into the social rhythms of your community.* Having identified such a person of peace, Jesus then says, "Stay there, eating and drinking whatever they give you, for the worker deserves his wages. Do not move around from house to house" (v. 7). This has become one of the greatest challenges to the church today. And yet we are called to humbly and graciously submit ourselves to the social rhythms, diet and practices of the community, rather than forcing them to submit to ours. We delight in the stories of Hudson Taylor and other great pioneers of nineteenth-century mission to China, and the way they shaved their heads and grew pigtails and tied them in topknots. We hear they wore Chinese dress and ate Chinese cuisine, practices that were considered scandalous in their time, and we consider them heroes. And yet judging our neighbors and refusing their offers of hospitality have become standard practice in many churches today.

- *Heal the sick.* Remember, the miracles and the parables were signs that the universal reign of God had broken into the world. They were authentications that Jesus is Messiah and Lord. We too are instructed to make signs of God's reign clear today. These will include social justice, joy, beauty, peace and mercy. But they will also include healing the sick and the deliverance of those held captive by spiritual forces, addictions and destructive patterns of behavior.

- *Announce the universal reign of God.* This is the most impressive aspect of the mission of Luke 10. When the disciples are instructed to declare their message, it is this: "tell them, 'The kingdom of God has come near to you'" (v. 9). Having previously announced the shalom of God—his mercy and favor in setting all things right—the disciples must now tell those they've broken bread with and whose hospitality they have accepted, the kingdom of God *is near!* Imagine a family in remote Tyre in Galilee or in coastal Joppa or in Beersheba in the south being told as they sit at their family's dinner table that the kingdom of God is near. For them, the kingdom or presence of God was only found in Jerusalem and even there only in the temple. And yet one of the spiritual practices of the earliest followers was to identify the grace and power of God in revealing his reign and universal rule to be present everywhere, always.

These ancient practices call us into place. They insist we live out our faith not in church worship services and Bible study groups alone, but in relationship with our neighbors, in compassionate, humble collaboration with others and focused on the glory of the triune God. One of my great inspirations in the discussion about a reengagement with place is the Kentucky writer and pastoralist Wendell Berry. He has written a meditation on the importance of long-term connection to the land and the intimate relationship between the earth and human culture:

> For many years now my walks have taken me down an old fencerow in a wooded hollow on what was once my grandfather's farm. A battered galvanized bucket is hanging on a fence post near the head of the hollow, and I never go by it without stopping to look inside. For what is going on in that bucket is the most momentous thing I know, the greatest miracle that I have ever heard of: it is making earth. The old bucket has hung there through many autumns, and the leaves have fallen around it and some have fallen into it, and the fallen leaves have held the moisture and so have rotted. . . . This slow work of growth and death, gravity and decay, which is the chief work of the world, has by now produced in the bottom of the bucket several inches of black humus. I look into that bucket with fascination because I am a farmer of sorts and an artist

of sorts, and I recognize there an artistry and a farming far superior to mine, or to that of any human. . . .

It collects stories too, as they fall through time. It is irresistibly metaphorical. It is doing in a passive way what a human community must do actively and thoughtfully. A human community, too, must collect leaves and stories, and turn them to account. It must build soil, and build that memory of itself—in lore and story and song—that will be its culture. These two kinds of accumulation, of local soil and local culture, are intimately related.[19]

13

# The First Page of the End of Despair

*We are living in troubled times and people have
become bothered and bewildered. When [this happens]
great caution is needed because our instinctive
response is scapegoating and death-dealing.*

ANN MORISY

On November 18, 1978, in Jonestown, Guyana, just over nine hundred
members of the People's Temple drank grape Flavor Aid laced
with potassium cyanide, liquid valium and other drugs to commit
the largest mass suicide in history. In fact, until September 11,
2001, it was the single greatest loss of American civilian life in a
nonnatural disaster. As is well known, the leader of the cult was
Rev. Jim Jones, who lives on in our memories in photographs
wearing dark sunglasses and pale safari suits, seated on a throne
in the jungles of South America. These images have come to epit-
omize our stereotype of the insane cult leader. But interestingly,
Jones and the People's Temple didn't begin this way. Far from it, in
its earlier days in the 1950s in a racially mixed neighborhood in
Indianapolis, the People's Temple was an exciting and radical Pentecostal church. It founded social services all over the city, in-

cluding an integrated orphanage, and a free restaurant and social
service center in the Temple's basement, feeding thousands of
homeless people every month and highlighting the prevalence of
poverty and social needs in the city.

In those days Jones campaigned for the racial integration of
churches, restaurants, the telephone company, the police department,
a theater, an amusement park and the Methodist Hospital. After
swastikas were painted on the homes of two African American families, Jones personally walked the neighborhood comforting African
Americans and counseling white families not to move, in order to
prevent white flight. He set up stings to catch restaurants refusing
to serve African American customers. He also wrote to American
Nazi leaders, then leaked their responses to the media. When Jones
was accidentally placed in the black ward of a hospital after he collapsed in 1961, he refused to be moved and began to make the beds
and empty the bedpans of black patients. Political pressures resulting from this caused hospital officials to desegregate the wards.

More than that, Jim and his wife, Marceline Jones, personally
adopted children of different races and cultures, becoming known
as the "rainbow family." They adopted three children of Korean
American ancestry, in line with Jones's pleas to Temple members to
adopt orphans from war-ravaged Korea. They also adopted a
daughter who was partly of Native American descent, and they
became the first white couple in Indiana to adopt a black child,
James Warren Jones Jr.

But these were the segregated 1960s, so the Joneses and the
members of the church often experienced harassment and threats.
Marceline was once spat upon while she carried Jim Jr. in the
street. On more than one occasion a swastika was painted on the
wall of the Temple or a gunshot was fired toward the building. A
stick of dynamite was left in the Temple's coal pile, and after a
threatening phone call a dead cat was thrown at Jones's house. All

this badly affected Jones, adding to his growing paranoia and contributing to his decision to move the congregation to San Francisco in the early 1970s.

Soon, he began deriding traditional Christianity, rejecting the
Bible as being white men's justification to subordinate women and
subjugate people of color, and stating that it spoke of a "Sky God"
when there was no God at all. He began claiming to be the reincar-
nation of Mohandas Gandhi (who was still alive when Jones was
born) as well as Jesus of Nazareth, Buddha and Vladimir Lenin. His
paranoia and megalomania only increased in San Francisco, and he
managed, remarkable as it sounds, to convince over one thousand
members of his congregation to follow him all the way to a primitive campsite in the Guyana jungle. Why didn't his family and
congregation see the trajectory he was on? And especially, why did
they drink the Flavor Aid?

## BOTHERED AND BEWILDERED

The expression "drink the Kool-Aid" is shorthand for anyone who
believes unhealthily in something, who invests their life entirely in
some campaign or project, whether religious, political or otherwise.
In the case of the People's Temple, the congregation went from
being a socially progressive, missional Pentecostal church, having
significant impact on their city, to the quintessential renegade cult.
One of the significant elements in this dramatic and relatively quick
decline was the paranoia Jones was able to generate within his followers. While there was evidence that the church and the Joneses
were the objects of derision and exclusion in Indianapolis, by the
time they relocated to progressive San Francisco all that changed.
Feted by political leaders and enjoying a reputation as the church
of the future, the People's Temple was becoming one of America's
first and most successful megachurches. But Jones amped up the
end-times rhetoric, warning his people that America was turning

on them. He proclaimed Jonestown to be "socialist paradise" and a
sanctuary from what he called America's creeping fascism. He
ranted about corporations or the multinationals getting much
larger, and their influence growing within the government. He declared the United States to be a racist nation. All this was against
the backdrop of enormous social upheaval in America at that time,
which only reinforced the sense of chaos, perversion and the lack
of control experienced by members of Jones's congregation. As
David Frum says of the era: "The 1970s were America's low tide.
Not since the Depression had the country been so wracked with
woe. Never—not even during the Depression—had America's pride
and self-confidence plunged deeper."[1]

America's fight against the spread of communism in Southeast
Asia and the subsequent protests about the Vietnam War,
strengthened by television images showing the brutality and point-
lessness of war, fostered the sense of an emerging anarchism in the
United States. The women's movement pushed for the rights of
American women in the workplace and the home, as well as challenging long-held stereotypes of women. A sexual revolution was
also taking place, in which taboos were broken and traditional
gender roles were being renegotiated. Victor Bockris says,

> The 1976-80 period, in which the Southern Democrat Jimmy
> Carter occupied the White House, was the most permissive
> period in the history of the United States. Never before had
> so many people taken so many drugs; never before had so
> many people had so much sex with so many different kinds
> of people in so many ways.[2]

Soon, Jones was describing America as an evil place where they
would be no longer safe. In Jonestown, Guyana, he began preaching
about "revolutionary suicide" as a way of protesting the conditions
of an inhumane world, a way to avoid the torturing of babies and

seniors, and a way to control the manner of their deaths, which Jones eventually believed was inevitable.

In her charming English way, Ann Morisy would say the members of the People's Temple had become "bothered and bewildered."[3] In her book of that title Morisy claims we are living today in times of similar uncertainty and upheaval. She writes of our age as being "dystopian," an expression used by such science fiction writers as Aldous Huxley in *A Brave New World* and George Orwell in *Nineteen Eight-Four*. A dystopia is the opposite of utopia, a fundamentally broken society often characterized by dehumanization, totalitarian governments, environmental disaster or other characteristics associated with a cataclysmic decline in society. Nowhere is dystopia better portrayed than in Stanley Kubrick's film of Anthony Burgess's *A Clockwork Orange*. Run through the sieve of Jim Jones's mental state, promises of American dystopia sent a thousand people into the jungle to drink cyanide. But Ann Morisy's point is that the beginning of the twenty-first century brings with it similar fears. The global financial crisis, the war in Afghanistan, the age of terror, skyrocketing unemployment, America's fiscal cliff and debt ceiling fears, massacres in US schools, the dashed hopes of the Arab Spring, simmering racial tensions—the list goes on and on. The first decade and a half of this new century seems every bit as bothersome and bewildering as anything the People's Temple were experiencing. But what makes religious groups—and particularly Christian groups— vulnerable to extreme reactions to the appearance of dystopian conditions is our narrative of rescue and our hope of salvation. I'm not saying God's promises to rescue and save his people are unhealthy, but as Ann Morisy points out, they can be twisted in extremely unhelpful ways:

> Salvation is not to be confused with escape. Religious assurance of eternal safety that protects the faithful from earthly

struggle is a heresy. But it is a very tempting heresy. Christians have to be wary of disdain for a world "gone wrong," especially when this combines with the desire to escape.[4]

I agree. In dystopian and confusing times Christians can be dangerously inclined toward promises of flight or temptations to fight. When we are bothered and bewildered we are at risk of escapist, self-serving theological strategies. Jim Jones and the People's Temple might be the most extreme case, but when you hear conservative Christians today expressing anxiety about their government and fears about the need to "take back" their nation, you can see how the fight-or-flight mechanism still affects us. Such escapist responses are rooted in a church-world dualism. When people become anxious and uncertain about the world around them, it is tempting to hunker down and believe the end-times rhetoric of televangelists, or alternatively to rise up and demand we fight against presumed dictators or the objects of bizarre conspiracy theories. It is disconcerting to feel the world is changing and you are being left behind, or worse, feeling as though the world has become antagonistic toward you. It feels hopeless. What the bothered and bewildered need more than anything in the midst of social change and upheaval is *hope*. The impact of secularization, the disintegration of Christendom and the shift in social norms has led many Christians to wonder what their place in Western society looks like. They are convinced of their Christian faith but struggle to understand what role Christianity plays in such a post-Christian culture. In search of such hope, Ann Morisy suggests we need to work hard to avoid two common mistakes:

1. The assumption that it is possible to impose solutions on people as a method of rekindling hope.

2. The habit of thinking in terms of "them and us."[5]

We see both of these responses in the church today. There is a general giving in to the powerful temptation that we can legislate others to maintain their commitments to our values or beliefs. And yet despite decades of attempts by the church to use political and legal processes to impose our solutions on our culture, the impact has been negligible. Likewise, them-and-us thinking has been rife throughout the church. Not only has it been expressed in glaring ways in the People's Temple or David Koresh's Branch Davidians in Waco, Texas, it can be seen in more socially acceptable ways in the objectification of others, thinking in clichés and stereotypes, and the caricaturing of enemies. Such a dualistic outlook undergirds and betrays an excarnate impulse and ultimately manifests in unhealthy ways. Says Walter Kania,

> In the U.S., there is an unrelenting drive of the radical religious right to take control of the government, the courts and the system of education. . . . Its authoritarian, power-based efforts to impose its agenda onto others and onto the culture of the US is a case-study and a prime example of unhealthy religion. It has more in common with the Islamic Taliban than with the teachings of its non-militant founder.[6]

## HEALTHY RELIGION

Identifying the differences between healthy religion and unhealthy versions is not that difficult. Any quick brainstorming session will lead to a list under each heading that might include some of the elements found in table 13.1.

It's obvious to us that unhealthy religion is abusive and manipulative, especially when we see it in stark examples like Jonestown or Waco. Perhaps it is a little more difficult to identify it in more socially acceptable versions in churches across America today, where total withdrawal and isolation are not required, but finger pointing, backbiting and self-righteous indignation are regular occurrences. What should be clear though is that unhealthy religious faith draws its strength chiefly from having an enemy (e.g., secular America, overbearing government, liberal Christianity), an alternate story that threatens the existence of the faithful. Further, it manipulates its people to make a stand against this evil.

**Table 13.1. Traits of healthy and unhealthy religions**

| Healthy Religion | Unhealthy Religion |
| --- | --- |
| Is concerned with the pursuit of God | Is concerned with things to avoid |
| Measures godly qualities | Measures quantities (of giving/service, etc.) |
| Finds our identity in grace | Finds our identity in behavior |
| Expands life | Constricts life |
| Results in transformation | Simulates holiness |
| Seeks wisdom | Seeks argument |
| Keeps learning | Maintains blind spots |
| Promotes rejoicing | Promotes suspicion |
| Releases | Suppresses |
| Welcomes | Isolates |

We see it today in the fanatical activities of Westboro Baptist Church in Topeka, Kansas, where Pastor Fred Phelps leads his congregation (composed mainly of family members) in a unique version of unhealthy religion—the picket line. Most people know of picketing as a legitimate form of protest, intended to draw the public's attention to a certain cause in a peaceful fashion. They might have seen it employed by trade unionists trying to prevent dissident members of their union or nonunion workers from working (by "crossing the picket line"). The Westboro Church uses it to express their views that other religions, including some other Christian churches, are "Satanic frauds preaching Arminian lies" and primarily to strongly condemn homosexuality. It is estimated they picket approximately six locations every day, including many in their hometown of Topeka. On Sundays, up to fifteen churches may receive pickets. The group travels nationally to picket the funerals of gay victims of murder or people who have died from complications relating to AIDS and other events related or peripherally related to homosexuality. The church claims to have participated in over 41,000 protests in over 650 cities in all 50 states since 1991, costing them an estimated $250,000 a year. In other words, the *primary* activity the members of Westboro Baptist Church must commit themselves to is an entirely combative one. Although it is a physical activity, it is nonetheless insidiously excarnate. Without involvement in anyone else's life, they feel free to make the most explosive and hurtful comments to them, often when they are at their most vulnerable. While picketing a funeral is much worse than breaking up with someone on Facebook, they're both lousy excarnate things to do.

Like Jonestown or Waco, it is tempting to think Westboro is only an extreme example and doesn't represent common church practice, but think about how often you've heard Christian rallies being described as "sending a message" to the world, or the need for the church to "defend" itself against some cultural trend. Try typing "take a stand for Christ" into your search engine. You'll be flooded with examples of similarly unhealthy religion. For example, on his website, Don Koenig expresses the paranoia of many when he writes,

Things are about to change radically in this country and in the world and it is going to happen much sooner than you might think. If you stand for nothing in America then for Christ's sake what makes you think that an antichrist spirit will not take over America? . . .

The symptoms of this are already evident. We now have an antichrist government that our "Christian" people actually helped to elect. We have sexual perversion being taught in our government indoctrination centers called schools because Christians will not take a stand against government sponsored perversion. The God ordained covenant of Marriage is being destroyed and the polls say that the majority of Christians now approve of same sex marriage??

Homosexuality with their filthy lifestyle will help spread super-germs to the general population. AIDS and MERSA is just the start of it. Wait until the super-germs from India spread here to these immune compromised incubators and feces wallowers. This homosexual practice was never acceptable in civil society because it cannot be allowed if civil society is to survive.

Many people are on drugs and drug warlords run your big cities. The traffickers have corrupted most everything for money including your government. We have the highest incarceration rate in the world and very few people that commit crimes even go to prison. Drug enforcement is also creating a police state in front of your eyes. Wake up! America is becoming increasingly wicked and it is a powder keg. The riots can start at any time.[7]

Koenig concludes this rant with a challenge for Christians to get serious, to abandon self-indulgence and greed and "take a biblical stand on the issues for Christ's sake!"[8] As I write this, that post had received nearly one hundred comments, all supporting Koenig's views in one form or another. I don't quote Mr. Koenig as the most influential or important blogger in this vein, although he's certainly one of the more colorful, but his post so perfectly illustrates the anxiety of unhealthy religion in America today. The language of "taking back" is entirely combative and expresses the two temptations Ann Morisy warned us of earlier: assumption that we can impose our preferred solutions on people, and thinking in terms of "them and us." It assumes the physical distance, relational disengagement and objectivism we have already explored.

So, what then does healthy religion look like? Ann Morisy refers to the work of Ron Sebring in defining it.

- Healthy religion does not indoctrinate, but teaches people to think for themselves.

- Healthy religion invites us to be humble about what we believe and what we know.

- Healthy religion does not invest in negativity; it does not major on what it is against but rather on what it is for.

- Healthy beliefs stay in tune with reality, never filling in gaps for what we do not know.[9]

In 2006, the Church of England commissioned the *Faithful Cities* report on urban life and faith. The primary concerns of the Commission were the issues of how people live together and what makes a place good to live in. The purpose of their report was to also explore how churches can play a part in human flourishing and urban regeneration. It found, in part, that healthy, life-giving faith that contributes to the thriving of the city will have the following hallmarks:

- *It will enlarge our imagination*: by setting the story of our lives in the framework of a much larger story than ourselves which gives our life coherence, meaning, purpose and direction.

- *It will teach and encourage the practice of wisdom and holiness*: finding our happiness and fulfillment is about coming to a right understanding of who we are, and what it means to be mature human beings in terms of vulnerability as well as potential.

- *It will open us up to the new*: while religion continues to be a profoundly important vehicle for personal and community identity it also embraces a humility borne of the awareness that our knowledge is partial—we see through a glass only darkly. Healthy religion gives confidence to embrace the stranger and insights that are available from those with a different experience of life.

- *It will deepen our sympathies*: it unlocks our compassion because it sees the whole of humankind sharing in a common unfolding story.[10]

Several of these ideas were explored in chapter twelve on the role of churches in their cities. For our purposes here it is important to note that healthy religion is embodied, placed and regenerative. It is lived out large and in the open. It contributes practically to the world and the communities around it. It practices hospitality, works for a more just world and cares for the environment. It sees its primary mission as being to alert others to the peaceable, merciful, gracious, universal reign of God through Christ. Those who have been blessed with a healthy religious outlook see themselves as a blessing to their community, drawing encouragement from Jeremiah 29:7: "Seek the peace and prosperity of the city to which I have carried you into exile. Pray to the LORD for it, because if it prospers, you too will prosper." Even in exile and dislocation it is possible to embrace our common cause and see something of the good in an alien place, rather than seeing others as enemies or threats. In *The City of God*, Augustine imagined two cities: the "heavenly city" and the "earthly city," and suggested that Christians are called to live between the two, attempting to embody a vision of the ultimate and transcendent amid the immanent. This world, though riven with contradictions, is still undeniably the place of divine deliverance and covenant. In her beautiful poem "Dreams Before Waking," American poet Adrienne Rich expresses the hope of a fully engaged person, ready and willing to act, to serve, to embody change:

What would it mean to live
in a city whose people were changing
each other's despair into hope?—
You yourself must change it.—
What would it feel like to know
your country was changing?—
You yourself must change it.—
Though your life felt arduous
new and unmapped and strange
what would it mean to stand on the first
page of the end of despair?[11]

In the great and vast story of humankind, as the followers of Jesus we can rightly see ourselves standing on the first page of the end of despair, and contributing to the writing of the rest of human history.

# 14

# Getting There

*Future shock is the shattering stress and disorientation*
*that we induce in individuals by subjecting them*
*to too much change in too short a time.*

ALVIN TOFFLER

**W**e need to move from unhealthy, excarnate religion to the approach
we see in the example of Jesus: a healthy, life-giving, dynamic
commitment to serve and glorify God in all we do. Getting there
won't be easy, especially when the dualistic world of "them and us"
is so embedded in our religious culture. Might I suggest a few skills
I think are necessary for the process?

## REFLECTIVE PRACTICE

In *Through Painted Deserts*, Don Miller writes about the need to
leave home in order to rediscover it. He says, "Everyone has to
change, or they expire. Everyone . . . has to leave their home and
come back so they can love it again for all new reasons."[1] He goes
on to explore the need for us all to act our way into a new way of
thinking. His book is a travelog of his journey across America, a
grand adventure that forced him to rethink his values and pri-

orities and return home a changed man. This process of reflecting on action, but also reflecting on the future in light of our action, is a key skill for overcoming the worst impulses of unhealthy religion. It is called reflective practice and was defined by one of its earliest proponents as "the capacity to reflect on action so as to engage in a process of continuous learning."[2] Unhealthy religion results from leaders and churches that are not effective in such an action-reflection model of learning. They become stuck, and in their stuckness they fall into all kinds of manipulative and control-based tactics for ensuring assent. When bothered and bewildered about change, they revert to isolation, control and to the rehearsal of the same old patterns that got them stuck in the first place. In Miller's analogy, it's as if these churches can never leave home.

When social change is rapid and continuous, churches can feel like there's little time to do anything but retreat or close down, or to react and attack. It feels as though we can't plan ahead, reassess strategy or discuss the implications of change. That often leads to defaulting to a pragmatism that reflects neither our values nor our beliefs. To stanch this unreflective pragmatism we need to find leaders who are willing to insightfully evaluate the issues of their context, ask meaningful and probing questions of the Bible and their theological tradition, and then continue to act, lead, choose and do. In brief, reflective practice is an essential skill that ensures leaders remain lifelong learners.

Donald Schön, one of the key thinkers in this field, wrote that he begins with the assumption

> that competent practitioners usually know more than they
> can say. They exhibit a kind of knowing-in-practice, most of
> which is tacit. . . . Indeed practitioners themselves often reveal
> a capacity for reflection on their intuitive knowing in the

midst of action and sometimes use this capacity to cope with the unique, uncertain, and conflicted situations of practice.[3]

In other words, church leaders, over time, develop a repertoire of images, ideas, examples and actions that help them know how to respond to challenging or demanding situations. This is a kind of *knowing in action*. It can be compared to an elite athlete, who doesn't have time to assess each situation he or she is confronted with, but has a type of artistic, intuitive reaction to it. The problem arises when that is the *only* kind of knowing exhibited by ministers and church leaders. It is reflexive, not reflective. When unusual or un-expected challenges are thrown at us, reflexive leadership doesn't work. When it doesn't, Schön says it forces us to engage in *reflection in action*. When situations of uncertainty, instability, uniqueness and conflict arise, as they are doing unremittingly these days, an internal conversation develops in our reflection in action. Schön says, "Doing extends thinking in the tests, moves, and probes of experimental action, and reflection feeds on doing and its results."[4] As Donald Miller found, it is in the doing that the opportunity for reflection and change arises. Good leaders look back on a pastoral encounter or a ministry event and realize that there is room for improvement in the way they approached it. It's when they know they need to do some more critical thinking about a particular issue or doctrine, or they need to take stock of their behavior or attitudes, that real reflective practice kicks in. This could be termed a kind of *reflection on action*, after the event.

But more than this, the ideal reflective practice for ministers is that which informs and enhances their future ministry. This is called *reflection for action* or reflection that looks forward. So the package of reflective practice for professionals includes knowing in action, reflection in action, reflection on action and reflection for action. When we embrace such a stance, we remain humble, teachable, open to change and compassionate. Donald Miller expresses this when he writes,

> I want to keep my soul fertile for the changes, so things keep getting born in me, so things keep dying when it is time for things to die. I want to keep walking away from the person I was a moment ago, because a mind was made to figure things out, not to read the same page recurrently.[5]

His own way of doing this, as a full-time writer, was to take a road trip across America in a Volkswagen van. It required action, risk, adventure. We can't all take such a trip, but we can all "leave home" in order to find our way back to what we love about it. It is in *doing*—embodied, enfleshed action—that the opportunity for real growth and learning arises. But it is as equally important that we develop the skill of humble, reflective practice, and that we embrace such reflection as whole churches or in leadership collectives, to ensure we overcome our fears and prejudices and blind spots. As Neil Sims writes,

> Without reflective practice we may be regurgitating the ministry much as we learnt when we were first ordained, almost oblivious of the huge changes happening in the world around us. Others sharing in our ministry may recognize that we really stopped learning when we left theological college.[6]

## Systemic Thinking

You've probably heard the expression, "If the only tool you have is a hammer, every problem looks like a nail." Unhealthy religion results from only seeing a small part of the overall complexity of life and faith, and from thinking there's only one (usually quite simple) solution to the problem. For some the solution is charismatic experience, for others it's Reformed Bible teaching. For yet others it's social justice, and others again it's church planting. But life is not so simple, and the challenges of living in the secular age are daunting and baffling. As much as we wish the solutions were simple and straightforward, in fact there are no magic bullets. A more systemic approach recognizes the complexity and richness of life, knowing that everything interacts with and affects the things around it. Systems thinking takes this interdependence into account. It acknowledges that things, events and people cannot be understood or addressed in isolation from the many other parts that comprise the whole. If we think we can *teach* our congregations the way out of whatever situation we face, we are naive, although knowledge, biblical thinking and good theology will be part of the answer. If we think effective leadership simply involves the setting of goals and the employment of capable staff, we will find ourselves in the same dilemma. If we focus entirely on the needs of the poor, we see only half the problem. If we think that strengthening the nuclear family is the primary solution, we ignore vast parts of the system to our peril. In an age of disengagement, displacement and dystopia we need leaders who can stand back far enough to see the whole, or at least enough of the whole to lead us humbly, graciously and caringly into an embodied, whole-of-life kind of discipleship. As Ann Morisy says,

> The great virtue of systems thinking is that it safeguards against two troublesome dynamics that gain momentum when people are anxious—the urge to blame and the urge to separate into "them and us." . . . Systems thinking resists blaming because of the recognition that when something goes wrong, the interconnectedness of our world means that the problem belongs with the system and not with an individual or group of individuals.[7]

## NONANXIOUS LEADERSHIP

Leaders who engage in reflective practice and systemic thinking will be nonanxious leaders. In fact, anxiety in leaders is the greatest indicator of unhealthy religion. The term *anxiety* is derived from the Greek word meaning "to choke" or to cause pain by squeezing. It was related to the word used for neck rings and nose rings worn by slaves. We get the English words *anger*, *angst* and *angina* from the same root. The negative effects of anxiety are well known—it is repressive, reactive and infectious. Like the restrictive, tightening word from which it comes, anxiety constrains us and forces us into controlling, fear-based behavior. Unfortunately, as Peter Steinke says, "Most people are interested in relieving their own anxiety rather than managing the crisis or planning for a clear direction. Their primary goal is anxiety reduction not congregational renewal."[8]

Anxious leadership dissipates the energy in any group. Its contagious effect leads people to pull in different directions, to alienate others and to blame their opponents. The Bible expresses it powerfully in this word picture: "Like a city whose walls are broken through is a person who lacks self-control" (Proverbs 25:28). A church led by anxious leaders has no internal sense of self or no collective purpose. Like the People's Temple or David Koresh's Branch Davidians, people are controlled by threats and social manipulation.

Maintaining a nonanxious presence in dystopian times does a number of things. It keeps the center of control within oneself rather than attempting to control others or the situation. It has a far more positive effect on other anxious people. Note the calming effect a controlled parent has on a tantruming child. It results in less friction, more imagination and healthier functioning. In fact, studies suggest that the regulation of reactivity when relating to others can be itself as infectious as anxiety-making behaviors. In times of enormous social change, Christian communities themselves need to be a calming, anxiety-relieving presence in their neighborhoods, but they are far less likely to be able to do this while they are led by anxious leaders.

Nonanxious leaders do the following things:

- They manage their own natural reactions.

- They use knowledge to suppress impulses and control automatic reactions.

- They keep calm and allow for conversation and reflection.

- They are observant (especially of themselves and their reactions).

- They tolerate uncertainty, frustration and pain.

- They maintain a clear sense of direction.

In *Congregational Leadership in Anxious Times*, Peter Steinke recommends a number of areas to work on our capacity to regulate our own anxiety and reactivity. They are:

*1. Know your limits and the limits of others.* Knowing your own and others' limits means developing a clear understanding of where "I" ends and someone else begins. In order to achieve this, leaders need to be able to define themselves authentically, rather than adapting to please others or defining themselves against others. It will also involve respecting the rights of others to be the way they are, yet refusing to allow others to violate or intrude on your own rights.

*2. Have clarity about what you believe.* Nonanxious leaders hold a clear set of convictions, values and beliefs, while also being frank and open about those things that are not worth "dying for" or about which they don't yet have certainty.

*3. Stand firm in the face of strong reactions.* Those who stand firm in the face of strong reactions are not bullheaded or stubborn. Instead, they know where they stand and what they believe in the face of disapproval and refuse to give in for the sake of harmony when it is a matter of principle.

4. *Stay connected to others, despite it all.* Nonanxious leaders maintain a nonreactive presence with people who are reacting to them (whether they are being verbally attacked or avoided, or having their viewpoint minimized, etc.). They resist the impulse to attack or cut off those who react to them in order to appease them to dispel their own anger or frustration.[9]

## BETTER SOTERIOLOGY

Unhealthy religion of the Christian variety flourishes when we have an unbiblical understanding of soteriology. When we reduce the gospel of Jesus to a way of escape from this broken world, we exacerbate fight-or-flight responses in our congregations. David Bosch alerts us to the fact that evangelicals in particular seem to focus only on the salvation that comes through the death and resurrection of Jesus. While it's true that Jesus' work of defeating sin and death *saves* us, it is not true to say that is the totality of the gospel. Lesslie Newbigin writes,

> [The Gospel] is concerned with the completion of God's purpose in the creation of the world. It is not—to put it crudely—concerned with offering a way of escape for the redeemed soul out of history, but with the action of God to bring history to its true end.[10]

Indeed, the work of Christ saves us, but not to pluck us out of this world and ready us solely for the one to come. Christ has redeemed us in order that we might see our vocation as being sent into this world to serve and love and mirror the work of God in the world. When we embrace the gift of Jesus there is existential peace, the removal of shame and the presence of joy. But the other part of the gift of Jesus is that he shows us how to live in the here and now. Unhealthy religion is neurotic and fear based. It focuses so heavily on the hereafter that it makes its adherents petrified that they might by dint of some slight infraction lose the favor of God and the offer of salvation. A healthy Christian faith preaches and practices the breadth and depth and beauty of living as Jesus taught us to, of entering fully into the world we find ourselves in, and of cooperating with him in setting things right in preparation for the age to come. It is anchored in grace and has confidence in the trustworthiness of God.

Another aspect of soteriology that needs to be considered in shifting ourselves from unhealthy forms of religion to more healthy ones is a recovery of the idea of the scapegoat and the role it plays in the gospel story. Clearly, in the unhealthiest forms of religion, scapegoating and death dealing are central behaviors, as we have seen. Identifying the enemy and punishing them for their difference is a core practice. It not only asserts the dominance of the scapegoating group, it also reasserts their own sense of belief in their cause. It is destructive and generative at the same time, although what it generates is a sick form of belief.

Philosopher and anthropologist René Girard sought to understand the death of Jesus as a scapegoat and then to explore what effect this could have on the human practice of scapegoating today.[11] In examining the meaning of the death of Jesus, Girard saw that the atonement language used to describe the cross was drawn directly from the Hebrew tradition of the scapegoat. More than that, his earlier work led him to conclude that humans are essentially driven by desire for what another has or wants (he called this "mimetic desire"), and this desire naturally results in conflict between the desiring parties. As this conflict increases (he called this "mimetic contagion"), it puts society at risk. The result is that a scapegoat mechanism is triggered. This is the point where someone is identified as the cause of the trouble and expelled or killed by the group. Social order is restored as people are contented that they have solved the cause of their problems by removing the scapegoat, and the cycle begins again. Think of Nazi Holocaust or the Rwandan genocide as examples. Think of William Golding's classic novel *The Lord of the Flies*.

Remembering that Girard is a philosopher, not a theologian, he contends that this is what happened in the case of Jesus. He was identified by the religious authorities of his day as a threat to their position and authority, and they scapegoated him. But Girard goes further. He says the resurrection of Jesus from the dead proves him to have been innocent; humanity is thus made aware of its violent tendencies and the cycle is broken. His argument can be summarized as

- Jesus is the *final* scapegoat.

- The New Testament is on the side of Jesus, the scapegoat, making the Gospels unique because they help us to see the world through the eyes of the scapegoat, not simply as *scapegoaters*.

- Jesus refuses to let death be the final word and rises again triumphantly.

- The followers of the scapegoat enact the seizing of the scapegoat and his triumph over death in Eucharistic celebration.[12]

It would be Girard's conclusion that participation in a regular liturgy that celebrates Jesus as the final scapegoat should have the effect of freeing us from the desire to scapegoat others. Here is a perfect example of the use of an habitual practice to countermand the excarnate impulses of society today, if only the church would celebrate the Lord's Supper in such an enlightened fashion.

To so narrowly define the gospel as escape from this world, rather than exploring all the dimensions of the cross, can lead us directly toward unhealthy, isolationist, fear-based, excarnate religion. Rather, believing the gospel to free us from the social need to scapegoat, and send us into our world as agents of change and grace, will only be a good thing for us and for the world we're sent to.

## MISSIONAL HERMENEUTICS

Not only do we need to understand the gospel as broadly as possible, we need to recover the idea of reading Scripture for the purpose of living an embodied life, not simply for its own sake. Study for study's sake is always a concerning thing to me. It can lead us into excarnation. I'm not suggesting we shouldn't have a love of learning in general and of the Scriptures in particular, but we need to bear in mind the purpose for which the New Testament was written: to equip us to continue the apostolic witness that brought us into being as the church of Jesus. In that respect, devotional study is good insofar as it deepens our connection to Jesus, but it is an incomplete study of God's Word if it doesn't produce greater faithfulness and service in the real world.

Don't forget that the Branch Davidian sect spent most of their time studying the Scriptures, particularly the book of Revelation, albeit from the perspective of their leader, David Koresh. They were also enthusiastic students of the Scriptures, but their obsession with Koresh's "Seven Seals" theology, poring over Revelation and the Psalms in an attempt to understand the end times and make sense of their sinful world, led them to a very dark place. What is needed to keep biblical study healthy is a *missional hermeneutic*, a framework for interpreting the Bible in ways that equip, mobilize, nurture and sustain missional practice and service.

In a Bible study prepared for the 214th General Assembly of the Presbyterian Church (USA), Princeton missiologist Darrell Guder outlined a simple model for such a missional hermeneutic—that is, a way of studying and interpreting the Bible in light of or alongside missional incarnational living. He writes of the first Christian churches,

> They were called and empowered to be Jesus' witnesses (Acts 1:8), to "make disciples of all nations" (Matt. 28:19), to "pro-

claim the mighty acts of him who called you out of darkness into his marvelous light" (1 Pet. 2:9b). The New Testament Scriptures were written to equip them for that purpose.[13]

Guder here refers to the New Testament alone, but others have proposed a similar approach to the purposes for which the Hebrew Scriptures were written. Michael Goheen, for example, affirms that "the Old Testament scriptures were written to 'equip' God's people for their missional purposes." The New Testament also, he goes on to say, was written in order to "form, equip, renew the church for their mission in the world."[14] And James Brownson agrees with this missional purpose, although he casts that purpose somewhat more widely than simply the idea of equipping.

> The basic purpose of scripture, then, is to impart a shared identity to the people of God as a body called to participate in God's mission. This identity is grounded most centrally in the gospel, the good news that in the life, death, and resurrection of Jesus, we see the culmination of God's saving purpose for the world.[15]

That being said, Guder's model of missional hermeneutics is very useful in that it encourages us to interrogate the Bible with the following question: "How did this text equip and shape God's people for their missional witness then, and how does it likewise shape us today?"[16] In so doing, students of God's Word are encouraged to avoid study for the sake of study or as an intellectual pursuit in its own right. Far from it, says Guder, the New Testament was written out of missional engagement by its writers and first hearers, and must be read today in the same way. To assist us in that endeavor, he suggests five variations of that question that each student of Scripture must ask in interpreting the text for themselves: How does this text *evangelize* us (the gospel question)

*convert* us (the change question)

*read* us (the context question)

*focus* us (on God's inbreaking reign—the future question)

*send* us (the mission question)?[17]

As he says, "All five of these 'missional questions' may not be equally helpful in every text, and sometimes they will overlap. But with these questions in mind, we may discover . . . how God's Spirit continues to form and equip us for God's mission."[18]

In light of my example of the Branch Davidians, it should also be noted that we need to be reading widely and across all corners of the canon of Scripture to ensure we are engaging with God's Word systematically, and not selectively. Reading the Bible to discover what it reveals of the gospel, the need for change, the context (of its original hearers as well as ours), the future and the mission of God can't be a bad thing.

Going slightly further, Michael Barram pushes Guder's questions for sharper specificity and locatedness, attempting to take seriously the context in which the church reads the text. Some of his questions are

- Does our reading of the text challenge or baptize our assumptions and blind spots?

- How does the text help to clarify appropriate Christian behavior—not only in terms of conduct but also in terms of intentionality and motive?

- Does our reading emphasize the triumph of Christ's resurrection to the exclusion of the kenotic, cruciform character of his ministry?

- In what ways does this text proclaim good news to the poor and release to the captives, and how might our own social locations make it difficult to hear that news as good?

- Does our reading of this text acknowledge and confess our complicity and culpability in personal as well as structural sin?

- How does this text clarify what God is doing in our world, in our nation, in our cities, and in our neighborhoods—and how may we be called to be involved in those purposes?[19]

Of course, these questions are exactly the kinds of critically important missional questions that our social location has conditioned us to overlook or avoid. As George Hunsberger points out, Barram's questions

> provide a kind of critical criteria by which not only our questions but our conclusions as well are continuously tested. The accent on "our reading" serves to underscore the community's full responsibility for its "readings" and to remind the community that its readings are always open to being tested. As the community reads, it is being read![20]

## INTEGRITY AND MORAL FIBER

More than two hundred years since his birth President Abraham Lincoln continues to inspire us for his extraordinary leadership in one of the most trying times in American history. While not embodying every one of the skills exactly as I've explored them, he nonetheless provides an excellent example of a nonanxious leader who looked at the big picture, kept the end in sight and maintained fidelity to his text, the Constitution of the United States.

In *Team of Rivals*, historian Doris Kearns Goodwin describes Lincoln's counterintuitive decision to appoint the best and brightest to his Cabinet, even though they were also some of his greatest political rivals. Goodwin's book demonstrates Lincoln's capacity to listen to different points of view. He created a climate where Cabinet members were free to disagree without fear of retaliation. At the same time, he knew when to stop the discussion and after listening to the various opinions, make a final decision. When there was success, he shared the credit with all those involved, stating, "The path to success and ambition is broad enough for two."

Similarly, when mistakes were made by members of his Cabinet, Lincoln stood up for them. When contracts related to the war effort raised serious questions about a member of his administration, Lincoln spoke up and indicated that he and his entire Cabinet were to blame.

According to Goodwin, Lincoln treated those he worked with well. However, when he did get angry and frustrated, he found a way to channel those emotions. He was known to sit down and write what he referred to as a "hot letter" to the individual he was angry with, and then he would set the letter aside and not send it. If he did lose his temper, Lincoln would follow up with a kind gesture or letter to let the individual know he was not holding a grudge.

Lincoln understood the importance of relaxation and humor to shake of the stress of the day and to replenish himself for the challenges of the next day. According to Goodwin, Lincoln had a wonderful sense of humor and loved to tell funny stories. He encouraged a healthy atmosphere of laughter and fun in his administration. He also enjoyed going to the theater and spending time with friends.

But above all he had the inner strength to adhere to fundamental goals. In the summer of 1864, the war was not going well for the North. Members of Lincoln's party came to him and said that there was no way to win the war, and he might need to compromise on slavery. Lincoln held firm on the issue of slavery and turned away from their advice.

When the war ended and he won reelection, Lincoln did not focus on his achievements but rather, in his second inaugural speech, focused on bringing the country together as expressed in his famous words: "With malice toward none, with charity for all, let us strive on to finish the work we are in, to bind up the nation's wounds, to care for him who shall have borne the battle and for his widow and his orphan, to do all which may achieve and cherish a just and lasting peace among ourselves and with all nations."

Leo Tolstoy said of Abraham Lincoln that his greatness consisted of the "integrity of his character and moral fiber of his being." In dystopian times such as ours today, we need godly, missional leaders of similar moral fiber, willing to embody the values of the kingdom in nonanxious, generous, resolute ways.

# Epilogue

*Christ in Us and We in Christ*

*Our imitation of God in this life . . .*
*must be an imitation of God incarnate;*
*our model is the Jesus, not only of Calvary, but of*
*the workshop, the roads, the crowds, the clamorous*
*demands and surly oppositions, the lack of all*
*peace and privacy, the interruptions.*

C. S. LEWIS

🔁

**A**s we come to the end of our exploration of this excarnate culture and its effects on the church and its mission, we would do well to ask what it means to live out an embodied, placed, fully present expression of faith an age of disengagement, dislocation and dystopia. When all our cultural impulses are pushing us toward disembodiment and disconnection, how do we reverse them sufficiently to not only live out an incarnated version of the Christian faith as an end itself, but to also bring about meaningful cultural change? I think the answer to these questions has ecclesiological, liturgical, missional and pastoral implications.

## ECCLESIOLOGICAL IMPLICATIONS

Earlier, we noted C. S. Lewis's point that the incarnation is the central Christian miracle and raised questions about how we might take it seriously, not only for our own salvation but as a template for all Christian living—incarnational, embodied, situated. In seeking to adopt such an incarnational stance it is important that we acknowledge the fact that still today Jesus takes on flesh and dwells among us. In the New Testament writings of Paul it is clear that central to his understanding of the life of the church is the belief in the idea of "Christ in us." Jesus continues to inhabit flesh by being "in" his people, the church. Paul expresses this idea when sharing his own testimony: "I have been crucified with Christ and I no longer live, but Christ lives in me" (Galatians 2:20). This is not only an intensely personal experience for Paul but one he deeply desires for his churches. For instance, later in his letter to the Galatians he says, "My dear children, for whom I am again in the pains of childbirth until *Christ is formed in you*" (Galatians 4:19). Clearly, Christ being in us is not only something granted to us graciously by God, it is also something we must strive toward, offering more and more of our lives to the indwelling, enfleshed presence of God through Christ. To the Ephesians he says, "I pray that out of his glorious riches he may strengthen you with power through his Spirit in your inner being, so that Christ may dwell in your hearts through faith" (Ephesians 3:16-17). In fact, his shorthand phrase for the gospel of Jesus is the profound mystery now made known to all people, including the Gentiles: "Christ in you, the hope of glory" (Colossians 1:27).

The difficulty for those of us shaped by a highly individualized culture in the West is that we read these references as suggesting only a personalized, interior experience of God's love for *me*. Christ is in *me*, as distinct from in *us*! When we hear a preacher tell us that "Christ is in you," we appropriate the idea in an entirely individualized way and ask ourselves what it means for *me* that Christ is in me. Note how many of our worship songs and hymns express the same idea. For example, Adelaide Pollard's "Have Thine Own Way, Lord" (1907) was a declaration of her personal submission to God's will not to allow her to undertake missionary service in Africa as she'd desired. She wrote:

> Have thine own way, Lord! Have thine own way!
> Hold o'er my being absolute sway!
> Fill with thy Spirit 'till all shall see
> Christ only, always, living in me.

This is a highly personal expression of faith and submission. Pollard is writing about her internal struggle to come to terms with disappointment with God. That's fine as far as it goes, but Christians have been shaped by these lyrics. Because nowhere does the hymn suggest that submission to God's will might be a collective experience, it's easy for people to believe that "Christ in me" is an intensely private experience. What would it mean for us to pray that God would have his way in us, collectively? Furthermore, songs like Johnny Cash's "Wildwood in the Pines" reinforce the point. It contains the line, "I believe that Jesus loves me. I can feel it in my soul."[1] And Michael Card's reworking of the old song *Jesus Loves Me (This I Know)* includes this verse:

> Jesus loves me, this I know
> It's not just the Bible that tells me so
> I can feel it, feel it in my soul
> Jesus loves me, this I know.[2]

In songs like these, the truth of the gospel is determined by my personal inner feeling about it. Now, I'm not arguing that personal conviction and individual devotion have no place in the Christian church. But I am suggesting that when Paul wrote about "Christ in you, the hope of glory," he was thinking of the congregation as a whole. While I know this has individual implications, and such personalized responses are expressed in these songs, we overemphasize them to the exclusion of the corporate implications. Christ is in the church as a whole, not just in individuals. As Pete Ward says, "We should place significantly more emphasis on how our connection to Christ makes us part of the body, rather than the other way around."[3] Ward provocatively suggests that while we are ready to believe that the church is the body of Christ, we are terribly shy about believing that the body of Christ is the church. But it is true. Where is Jesus to be found on this planet but in an enfleshed form in the collective body of his people? We need to come to terms with seeing the whole church—global, local, intergenerational—as Christ embodied in this world.

If we wish to countermand the excarnate impulses of our world, we need to come to terms with the biblical understanding that Christ is present in the world through his people, collective, rooted, embodied, practical, actional people.

### THE LITURGICAL IMPLICATIONS

Resisting excarnation has liturgical implications as well. Charles Taylor says, "there is no way in which I will have a relation to God which is not in some way or other embodied."[4] He goes on to describe this as being like a poet searching for the right word. The poet knows the right word is there, somewhere, but until he or she finds it the process of expressing oneself through the poem is incomplete. Searching for the right word is a metaphor for needing to express our relationship to God physically. It's as if God (the right word) is out there, but we have to find a way to connect with him, to complete the sentence or the phrase. Taylor says that "the presence of the sacred could be enacted in ritual, or seen, felt, touched, walked towards (in pilgrimage)."[5] Alas, much of our

Christian ritual is highly personalized and inwardly sensed. Liturgy
is one of the ways we find "the right word" for God. Liturgy literally means "the work of the people." It is the collective practices
or rituals that the people of God undertake to unite themselves to
him and to each other. One of the ways we express our faith in the
truth that Christ is in us and we in Christ is through such collective rituals.

Recently I have rediscovered the beauty of the Lenten season. I
find it one of the most meaningful seasons of the Christian calendar.
Growing up Catholic I was conscious of the oddity of my mother
refusing to eat meat on Fridays during the lead up to Easter. It was
never explained to me why we could only eat fish, and as I became
a teenager I began to see it as legalistic or superstitious. That mat-
tered nothing to my mother. While she didn't impose the whole
sacrifice on her children, she herself fasted on Ash Wednesday and
Good Friday, having only one meal on those days. Then, not only
did she abstain from meat on Fridays, a fast we were obligated to
join her in, she also privately gave up something else as a sacrifice
for the full forty days.

As a young man my Christian conversion reshaped me as a fiery
evangelical and iconoclast. I rejected this practice altogether, only
to reengage with it in midlife. By then I had discovered the beauty
of the rhythm of the Christian calendar. I belong to a church that
hosts an annual Stations of the Cross art exhibition every Easter,
featuring work by both Christians and non-Christians. Walking
the Via Cruces from one depiction of Christ's suffering to the next
was a blessed experience, and it was not long until we rediscovered
Lent, an annual period of abstinence and sacrifice aimed at enriching the personal and collective bearing of our brokenness and
sin. Giving up something for Lent wasn't superstitious or legalistic
at all. It was an annual habit, an embodied practice that focused
my attention on the heaviness of my sin and made me yearn for

the freedom of grace that we celebrate on Resurrection Sunday. When one gives up a regular practice, like drinking coffee, eating chocolate or checking social media, there is naturally an equally regular twinge of desire throughout the day when I'd really feel like a latte or a Snickers bar or to log onto Facebook. During Lent, every time I feel that pang of desire, it triggers a commitment to pray, to confess sin and cry out to God. After nearly a month of this I would then spend a morning praying the Stations of the Cross, reengaging with the sufferings of Jesus, again reminding me of the weight and horror of human sin. Nothing prepares me to enjoy Easter Sunday quite like Lent and the Stations. Those of us who've abstained from chocolate for the month, crack open the biggest Easter eggs we can find, and coffee abstainers guzzle strong espressos. We are free in Christ! Hallelujah.

The Christian calendar was developed to ensure that Christians embraced an embodied rhythm to their lives, one that insisted that every year in the lead up to Easter we come face to face with the burden of our sin. Lent therefore became an annual trigger for the Christian community to reembrace repentance and the freshness of new life. But likewise, Advent became an annual trigger to yearn for the second coming, the hope of glory, the yearning for all things to be set right. Easter Sunday, Pentecost Sunday, Christmas Day—they each insist on an annual reengagement with different aspects of the Christian story. They are a kind of imposed alarm clock, a blaring reminder of our beliefs and a call to *act*. Whether it is through the Sunday service or giving up something for Lent or decorating our house or making pancakes, these traditional liturgical actions are prompts for a deeper and more enfleshed engagement with our faith in God. Clarissa Pinkola Estes says, "Ritual is one of the ways in which humans put their lives in perspective, whether it be Purim, Advent, or drawing down the moon. Ritual calls together the shades and specters in people's lives, sorts them out, puts them to rest."[6]

Of course, all liturgical action can become meaningless when done by rote, but today, thanks to excarnate pressures in society, ritual and liturgy are going out of vogue. If we are to resist these pressures, a rediscovery of liturgy, pilgrimages, symbols and practices will be essential. We noted earlier James K. A. Smith's helpful reminder that, first and foremost, we are "loving, desiring, affective, liturgical animals."[7] Driven more by desire than by knowledge, if we as Christians wish to please God we need to rightly order our desires in such a way as to give him the glory and honor in our lives. Smith also pointed out that we "don't inhabit the world as thinkers or cognitive machines. . . . [G]iven the sorts of animals we are, we pray *before* we believe, we worship before we know—or rather, we worship *in order* to know."[8] Smith points out how our lives are already shaped by liturgical triggers or practices that reinforce our desires, whether they be going to a shopping mall for entertainment, checking social media at regular intervals in our day or giving our all to a corporate job. He calls us to ask ourselves whether we're happy with Westfield or Facebook establishing those rituals, or whether we wish to take control ourselves and put around us a series of practices that reorder our desires, placing God as foremost.

As much as some might scoff at this practice these days, our parents' daily "quiet time" was such a ritual. Considered quaint today, it nonetheless established the Word of God as primary in their life. I'm not necessarily suggesting a return to that form, but I am asking what rituals shape your life by imposing prompts in your life to help you rightly reorder your desires. The quiet time did in fact do that for many generations. For devout Catholics, daily and weekly Mass does that, as do the rites of confessions and absolution. I fear that for evangelical Protestants there has been such an abandonment of bodily forms of worship and liturgy that we have thrown the baby out with the holy water (sorry). You see, liturgy doesn't only provide an avenue for us to honor or acknowledge God's worth, as important as that is; it is also a kind of imposed spiritual scaffolding that assists in developing resistance to our excarnate culture. As Lee Camp says, "To pray good prayers regularly, not in rote recitation but in earnest sincerity, opens one to profound renewal."[9]

Protestants today, influenced as they are by charismatic and Pentecostal forms of worship, have tended to reduce worship and liturgy to mere singing (in practice, rather than in theory). But the English word *worship* can be applied appropriately to both the ideas of homage and service. It's right that we sing adoration to God, paying homage to him, but it is empty if it is not accompanied by a life of service to match. Developing liturgical practices as ways of honoring God and building the framework for a life of rightly ordered desires is essential for effective discipleship. As Tom Sine says, "We will need to aggressively work for the re-monking of the church to enable followers of Jesus Christ to intentionally set the focus and rhythm of their lives out of biblical calling instead of cultural coercion."[10]

What could it look like if churches saw themselves more like monastic missionary orders, communities of encouragement, support and training we emerge from to live as Christians in the workplace and to which we return for reflection and renewal? In *The Faith of Leap*, Alan Hirsch and I refer to the Celtic rhythm of the cell and the coracle, the cell being the place of a monk's retreat, reflection, prayer and liturgy, and the coracle being the small fishing boat used by missionary monks to traverse the high seas.[11] Celtic missionaries oriented their lives around this rhythm—liturgy and mission, rhythm and chaos, safety and adventure. I am not proposing we necessarily comprise a literal monastic order but a group of comrades who will be bound to God and each other by a "rule," a set of common values, liturgies and commitments. In my own church, *Small Boat, Big Sea*, we have developed a simple rule or order to our communal life. It is summarized under the acrostic BELLS.

- *Bless*—we will bless at least one other member of our church and at least one other person in our neighbourhood every week. This will take different forms. We might write a letter, deliver a gift, say a word of encouragement, perform an act of service. But in essence we will commit ourselves to the weekly rhythm of performing acts of kindness and generosity.

- *Eat*—we will eat with at least one other member of our church and at least one other person in our neighbourhood every week. Sharing a table is the great equalizer in human relationships. Eating together breaks down barriers and promotes a healthy sense of solidarity. It models hospitality and fulfils the model presented in Luke 10 of sharing table fellowship with others. Further to that, our church eats together every Sunday night, each of us bringing a plate of food to share with the others. Also, we are divided into groups of three that meet weekly for mutual accountability, discipleship and nurture. Those smaller cells usually meet over a meal or coffee (my group meets for breakfast each week).

- *Listen*—we will commit ourselves weekly to listening to the promptings of God in our lives. Again, this will take different forms for different people. Some of us are very spiritually intuitive and hear from God in visions, pictures and other ecstatic experiences. Others of us make our weekly commitment to search out God's voice in less spectacular ways. We will ensure a weekly time of solitude to listen to God. We will take a prayer-walk, find time alone in a special place, use prayer beads, etc. These more liturgical expressions are essential as the spiritual scaffolding I mentioned earlier.

- *Learn*—we will read from the Gospels each week and

remain diligent in learning more about Jesus. Of course, we encourage our members to read the whole Bible and to have a regular rhythm of biblical study. But in our attempts to be a Jesus-centered collective, we emphasize a weekly exploration of the Gospel stories about him.

• *Send*—we will see our daily life as an expression of our sent-ness by God into this world. Earlier we looked at the dualism that has beset the mainstream church, a dualism that assumes that our life outside church is irrelevant to the extension of God's kingdom. At our church we are committed to looking for ways our daily lives can be expressions of our "sent-ness," our mission as agents of God's grace on this planet. This will include acts of hospitality and the just stewardship of our resources, as well as working for justice and striving for global peace.[12]

This rhythm, or set of commitments, isn't just our private, personal expression of our devotion to God. Our weekly love feast is conducted along the same BELLS rule, but at this time it is more like a liturgy. We gather and bless each other, speaking words of encouragement and affirmation over one another. Then we eat a shared meal together, during which we break bread and dip it in wine to celebrate Jesus' presence with us and to remember his sacrificial death on the cross. After the meal we spend time listening to God and sharing with each other anything we've heard God say to us during the week. Then we have a time of shared learning, rooted in the Scriptures. Finally, we leave time for people to share how they mirrored the work of God in their sentness that week. People talk about their work as healers or teachers or builders, and are affirmed for the efforts they have undertaken. In this way we try to break down the dualism that occurs in many churches, where our daily lives are completely irrelevant to our Sunday experience.

I don't share this as the ultimate way to do it but simply as one church's attempt to embrace liturgical and missional practices that help us reorder our desires. Lee Camp speaks of the need to resist cultural forces that countermand humble obedience to God. He writes specifically of prayer here, but the point can be applied to all regularly practiced liturgy, ritual or spiritual habit:

> The principalities and powers of marketplace and government, investment banking and economics, education and culture, all school us to balk at such an "out-of-control" lifestyle [of trust in God]. Cultural forces such as these incessantly foster an illusion of control—or perhaps more accurately, they deliberately foster a *delusion* of control. Prayer, on the other hand, schools us to revel in trust rather than "autonomy," to delight in godly submission rather than ruthless competitiveness, to find joy in dependence upon God rather than dependence upon our own paltry efforts at controlling the world around us.[13]

A similar community to ours can be found in the Faubourg Marigny neighborhood of New Orleans. There we find a missionary order called Communitas, an apostolic band living in intentional Christian community among the lost and the least of the city. They are a marvelous example of a fully embodied, placed people. As a missional community (well, three households, actually) they are committed to

- partnering with their neighbors in collective community transformation

- sharing with their neighbors a common pilgrimage toward Christ

- creating fresh expressions of biblical faith communities which are culturally relevant to their context

- empowering like-minded emerging leaders in fresh expressions and communities in their cities[14]

They do this by centering their lives around a common rhythm. Each member of Communitas agrees to (1) weekly prayer, Eucharist and journey with God through his Word, (2) weekly mentoring within the community, (3), a weekly learning community time, (4) a weekly gathering called Matthew's Table, in which all comers from the neighborhood are invited to join them for a fun night of food and conversation, (5) regular days out together, participating in the celebrations of the unique culture of New Orleans, and (6) regular times of serving the neighborhood through shared meals, "third place mission" and social service.

This "rhythm of life" is compulsory for all members, but access at the fringes of many of these gatherings and practices is open to all comers. I had the privilege of joining the folks at Communitas for a Matthew's Table gathering a little while ago and was deeply touched by their joy and their hospitality.

In Seattle, the Mustard Seed Associates, led by Tom Sine and Christine Sine, host an annual Lenten retreat designed to awaken a hunger for deeper intimacy with God. Based in part on Christine's book *Return to Our Senses*, it uses the simple things of everyday life—breathing, drinking a glass of water, running, picking up a stone or taking a photo—to open participants' senses to the God who shines through every moment and enlivens every creature.[15] Mustard Seed Associates also hosts an annual "Spirituality of Gardening" seminar, teaching people to rediscover the garden as a place where spirituality, sustainability and simplicity intersect. These retreats and seminars, and many others they host, are designed to draw people back into an embodied experience of God and an incarnational stance in the world today.

### THE MISSIONAL IMPLICATIONS

In chapter one we explored Zygmunt Bauman's idea that in the secular age, the *tourist* is the best metaphor for contemporary life.

Skimming over life, trying to remain unsullied by the reality of local customs or traditions, the tourist is insulated from the richness and messiness of life as experienced by the locals. It is a posture that dominates Western culture. As we are looking to find alternatives to disembodiment and disconnection, and to countermand them in our lives, perhaps a more fitting alternative metaphor to the tourist is the *pilgrim*. I touched on this briefly when looking at our connection to place a little earlier.

At first glance, the tourist and the pilgrim might look the same. They are both travelers, after all. But in fact their relation to their surroundings is entirely different.

- Tourists are escaping life; pilgrims are embracing it. Parker Palmer notes that, "In the tradition of pilgrimage . . . hardships are seen not as accidental but as integral to the journey itself."[16]

- Tourists are trying to forget; pilgrims are trying to remember. Pilgrimages are undertaken to awaken insight.

- Tourists are looking for bargains and photo opportunities, and aren't really *seeing* at all; pilgrims are seeking to come properly to attention.

- Tourists hate to be surprised; pilgrims believe that the surprises open them to new insight. As Kurt Vonnegut said, "Peculiar travel suggestions are tap dancing lessons from God."[17]

- Tourists wish to interact with the locals only sparingly; pilgrims rely on hospitality.

The stance of the pilgrim can rightly be compared with the experience of the disciples in Luke 10. Like pilgrims they are sent out to every town and village, not to glide over the communities they encounter but to enter into them, to accept their hospitality, to unearth the signs of the kingdom under their very noses. Jesus uses these "pilgrimages" as key teaching times, allowing his disciples to be surprised by what God does, to awaken their understanding of the kingdom and to broaden their awareness. In the same way, the missional implications of our desire to resist excarnation can be found in our vocation as pilgrims. While we might see ourselves as "passing through" this world, longing deeply for the world to come, we are to do so as rooted, placed pilgrims, not as acquisitive and covetous tourists.

I think we are called on to make and unmake the world God sends us to, in the same way as his first followers did. Walter Brueggemann notes that this is the role of much of the Old Testament material: a yearning for another world and an open disinterest in the existing world. He claims the psalmists often make and unmake their listeners' worlds in several ways:

1. The psalmists *make* a world that is intergenerational and *unmake* a world that is one-generational. Many psalms assert that what previous generations have done matters to the present generation, and what the present generation does is shaped by choices made in their past. The present generation both answers for and lives with the consequences of past actions. The same can be said of the preaching of the early church, as recorded in the Acts of the Apostles. A one-generational world absolutizes the present and diminishes a biblical worldview. It turns politics into an ideological project and silences ever-present suffering.

2. The psalmists *make* a world that is covenantally shaped and *unmake* a world that is devoid of any covenant. The psalms point to a sovereign Ruler who is bound to Israel in mutual loyalty. They regularly rehearse the indivisible nature of God and Israel working together on the extraordinary project of creating a just community. When the world is devoid of such a covenant, there is no call to the creative, costly, demanding, life-giving discipleship required by the kingdom of God.

3. The psalmists *make* a world that is morally serious and *unmake* a world that is morally indifferent. A morally indifferent world has no intense, ethical, political, economic agenda. Human life is reduced to matters of money, power, cleverness, influence, security and comfort. In such a world there are only commodities. But in a covenantal relationship with God, Israel is invited into an ongoing process of yielding, resisting, submitting, asserting and being judged and cared for by God.

4. The psalmists *make* a world that is politically demanding and *unmake* a world that is politically indifferent. The psalms are often not just religious statements but summon Israel to political discernments as a people in the world and to political decisions about how to arrange power in the world.[18]

All this making and unmaking is carried over into the New Testament mission, although now the kingdom of God is revealed and confirmed through Christ. We can add the evangelistic enterprise to Brueggemann's four goals and say, fifth, Christian *make* a world that acknowledges the lordship of Jesus and *unmake* a world that rejects, vilifies, scorns and attacks Jesus. Just as the psalmist has entered the fray and has committed himself to an intergenerational, covenantally shaped, morally serious and politically demanding new world, the church also commits itself to announcing the universal reign of God through Christ. Our mission is to partner with the triune God in making the world he is dreaming up, a counterworld, and in so doing to seek to unravel or subvert the dominant paradigm.

## PASTORAL IMPLICATIONS

"In troubled times, mission and pastoral care have to be allies," writes Ann Morisy.[19] When dealing with the effects of excarnation and secularization, the Christian community needs the skills to foster resilience and compassion. Ravi Zacharias referred to the need for "steadying the soul when the heart is under pressure."[20] Dreaming up new worlds sounds exciting enough, but often the outcome is not triumph and celebration, but dismay and anxiety. This is when missionally shaped pastoral care is needed. How are we to steady the soul under such circumstances?

I have found a meditation on Psalm 25 to be instructive here. The author of Psalm 25 has constructed this psalm as an acrostic, using the Hebrew alphabet, with an occasional irregularity, as its framework. It was clearly designed to be memorized and recited, and therefore it is more accurately approached as a teaching tool rather than a devotional psalm. Where some psalms are deeply personal expressions of faith or repentance by David (like Psalm 18; 34; 51), this psalm has a more general application. Its author is dreaming of a counterworld to the one around him and presents this acrostic to galvanize Israel's faith in difficult times. It provides a very helpful set of pastoral priorities for those of us seeking to lead Christian communities today, to steadying the soul when under pressure. In it, the psalmist prays to the Lord that he will be equipped and guided effectively for the task of making this new world. What does the psalm tell us about the life of those who embrace a new godly, righteous world, who battle injustice and struggle for peace?

First, we will endure suffering without shame.

> In you, LORD my God,
>> I put my trust.
> I trust in you;
>> do not let me be put to shame,
>> nor let my enemies triumph over me.
> No one who hopes in you
>> will ever be put to shame,
> but shame will come on those
>> who are treacherous without cause. (Psalm 25:1-3)

His enemies are rarely absent from any of the psalms ascribed to David. But he's not being paranoid, rather he is living with the reality of striving for a godly new world. Those who put their shoulder to the wheel and invest their lives in working to see the kingdom of God unfold will invariably incur the slings and arrows of those who prefer the arrangement of power the way it is. At times, David's enemies were those from other nations who saw Israel's rise as a threat. But often they were simply people who were ideologically as well as personally opposed to him. His commitment to the covenantal relationship with his sovereign God was an affront to some. His political and moral courage naturally upset those in power and with much to lose. Remember, this is a teaching psalm, not just a personal expression of frustration by a monarch under attack from neighboring nations.

How do our enemies "triumph over" us? In an excarnate world, such messy acts as feeding the poor and ministering to the marginalized might be considered shameful; choosing to live simply, to act generously, to sacrifice our time and energy in the pursuit of justice—these might seem in an excarnate culture to be absurd to the point of giving offense. These things might make enemies for us—whether neighbors and friends, or people in the halls of power, or the invisible, insidious advertisers whose excarnate values we are subverting.

How many times have you been laughed at when you mentioned that you're not chiefly motivated by money? How often have you felt ashamed because the prevailing opinion around you was racist or bigoted or without compassion? How often have we been scoffed at because we support racial reconciliation? Or women's rights? Or because we don't categorize certain people as illegal immigrants? Or worse? How many of us, having chosen to not take jobs in certain corporations or to not seek advancement in certain roles, have found ourselves disadvantaged by the system that prefers acquiescence?

I was once at a dinner party when all the couples present started comparing the amount of money they each spent of their new kitchen renovations. With pride, each couple was upping the ante by announcing they spent $20,000, $30,000, $50,000 on their kitchens. The owners of the home we were visiting spent $53,000 on their kitchen. As we were leaving I simply had to stick my head through the doorway to see what a $53,000 kitchen looks like. I confess it looked pretty nice, but it didn't actually do anything more than any modestly priced kitchen could do. A sink is a sink and an oven an oven. These couples, all Christians, had swallowed the lie and ended up believing that this use of money is perfectly reasonable. In fact, they were not living any differently, nor using their resources in any way differently, from their non-Christian neighbors.

The call of David, as one who is part of the making of a new world, is to put his hope in God and his covenant of love and mercy. This will not come without cost. We will suffer the alienation of sideways glances from those who live with this old world, but we will not be ashamed. Pastoral care that nurtures our capacity to endure suffering without shame is so important. People can be bogged down by suffering or rejection. They can resort to defensiveness and name calling, death dealing and the whole "them and us" thing. By contributing to the making of a new world we risk having our hearts broken. We court the possibility of being judged as naive. Church leaders must embrace their responsibility to foster self-discipline and a trust in the goodness of God if we are to not be imprisoned by such rejection or mockery. We need leaders to relieve us of the horror of shame in the midst of our suffering.

Second, we will require God's guidance.

Show me your ways, LORD,
    teach me your paths.

Guide me in your truth and teach me,
    for you are God, my Savior,
    and my hope is in you all day long.
Remember, LORD, your great mercy and love,
    for they are from of old.
Do not remember the sins of my youth
    and my rebellious ways;
according to your love remember me,
    for you, LORD, are good.

Good and upright is the LORD;
    therefore he instructs sinners in his ways.
He guides the humble in what is right
    and teaches them his way. (Psalm 25:4-9)

But what will protect us against self-righteousness and personal justification? What's to stop me from running around tsk-tsking at the amount people spend on their kitchen renovations when so many starve in this world? We don't want to become moral policemen, continually making judgments about others' choices. Nor do we want to be left to our own devices to make such judgments in our own lives. I believe that if I'm to be part of the unfolding of God's kingdom here on earth, I need more than my own insight or political ideologies or agendas to see me through.

Likewise with David. He doesn't want to be shamed or defeated by his enemies, but neither does he want to be the final arbiter of truth and righteousness, so he turns to his sovereign Lord and asks for guidance beyond his own experience. Let's be frank, sometimes those who have refused to embrace this old world and are partnered with God in the creation of a new one can appear arrogant and self-righteous. We can look down our noses at those still serving a consumeristic society. We can judge them by contemporary political ideologies and view them as right-wing or fundamentalists.

David's plea for guidance is both poignant and inspirational. He asks for guidance in a number of areas:

- *Wisdom in righteousness*. Note David's use of plurals: "Show me your ways . . . your paths" (v. 4). This goes beyond the self-interested requests to God for special guidance and invites him to grant us a foundational rightness that allows us "to distinguish good from evil" (Hebrews 5:14).

- *Persistence*. David's references to "all day long" (v. 5) and "My eyes are ever on the LORD" (v. 15) express his desire for God's strength and guidance for the long haul, for persistence and steadfastness in working for equity and justice in this world. We know that the ushering in of the kingdom is a long, slow process, and we need the capacity to endure.

- *Penitence*. By inviting God to keep us penitent we recognize our own sin and our own capacity for greed, violence, injustice, hatred and evil (v. 8). There is not one of us who is worthy to be called a child of God. We are infected with the same fallenness this unjust world suffers. And we must always be on guard against self-righteousness.

- *Obedience*. Verse 9 describes the attitude we should ask God for. Not an obedience that is embraced out of fear of retribution but out of humility or meekness. Ask God to make you biddable, teachable, gracious and godly.

  Third, we will depend on his forgiveness.

All the ways of the LORD are loving and faithful
  toward those who keep the demands of his covenant.
For the sake of your name, LORD,
  forgive my iniquity, though it is great. (Psalm 25:10-11)

We have not invented this new world that we are working toward. It was not our idea. It is God's mission and his plan, and we have been graciously invited to join him in it. For this we must remain in astonishment and wonder. That God chooses to partner with sinful, broken human beings is a continual source of amazement. There is no question that David is deeply aware of his own fallenness (v. 7) and the iniquity he was capable of. It is from this framework of sin and restoration that David's commitment to righteousness finds focus. He is not working to simply usher in some new ideological paradigm. His mission is deeply rooted in the experience of repentance and forgiveness. As a forgiven one he commits himself to living a life of creative righteousness, of obedience and godliness. Because he has encountered God's covenantal love, steadfast and sure, he must live out the covenant himself. His experience has informed his world-creating rhetoric. He cannot forget that a righteous, just God cares intensely about issues of justice and righteousness. As a follower of Yahweh, David cannot scuttle these concerns either.

He has acknowledged that God is good and upright (v. 8), and it follows that as a redeemed sinner, no matter how great his iniquity (v. 11), he must also be upright. I believe this is key.

Look at Titus 3:4-8. Here, Paul expresses the same idea. After a magnificent demonstration of the wonder of God's grace (vv. 4-7), he then counsels Titus to preach grace, "so that those who have trusted in God may be careful to devote themselves to doing what is good" (v. 8). In other words, doing what is good emerges from an experience of God's grace. We do not do good in order to earn God's favor or to impress him with our hard work and diligence. Rather, when we have been set free from guilt by God's unending forgiveness, we are free indeed to serve the poor and preach the gospel. As Marjorie Kempe once claimed she heard Jesus say to her in a vision, "More pleasing to me than all your works, and all your prayers and all your penances is if you would truly believe that I love you."[21] This isn't some form of pietistic individualized faith. It's when we finally let go of our guilt and our shame, and accept

Jesus' love that we are set free to serve others fully.

Fourth, we will trust in God's blessing.

The psalm begins with a declaration of trust (v. 2), which finds resonances throughout the passage (vv. 5, 8-10, 14). David will wait. He will wait upon God. Pastoral leadership strengthens and nurtures us to trust and abide in God. When the forces of globalization, economic rationalism, consumerism, racism and greed seem too much to bear, we must trust that this is not the final word. David is surrounded by enemies trying to put him to shame, but he will wait and trust in God for his vindication. He, in God's strength, shall overcome. Serene but active trust is a powerful force.

I think that's why Martin Luther King's "I Have a Dream" speech is so powerful, because it begins with him telling his audience about an unsuccessful assassination attempt on his life. He talks slowly and deliberately about how close the assassin's knife came to killing him. He acknowledges, as David does, that he is beset by enemies on every side. But he also declares, powerfully and dramatically, that he doesn't care. He has no concern for his own safety because he has been to the mountaintop. He has looked over the other side and seen a day when God's hand will rule, where justice for all will reign. His vision, his dream, of this utopian time sustains him in times of danger. So it is with the author of Psalm 25. He has had a dream:

> Who, then, are those who fear the LORD?
>     He will instruct them in the ways they should choose.
> They will spend their days in prosperity,
>     and their descendants will inherit the land.
> The LORD confides in those who fear him;
>     he makes his covenant known to them.
> My eyes are ever on the LORD,
>     for only he will release my feet from the snare.
>         (Psalm 25:12-15)

It's a delightful dream of a time when God will confide gently in his people, a time when humankind will be God's personal friend, his closest confidante. It will be a time when all prosper and care for the land, and where God's covenant is fulfilled, a covenant of justice and peace.

Is that your dream too? Never give up on the fight for the kingdom. We have tasted the truth and we cannot get the taste out of our mouths. We cannot go back. Only forward. We must stay focused as people who will help unmake the world that claims supremacy and offers nothing. We must remain part of radical communities of faith that keep offering up God's promises and keep demonstrating resonances of what God intends for human society.

Have no shame. We are right because God is right.

Rely on God's guidance, not our own political wisdom.

Lean heavily on God's grace.

And trust, wait and dream and keep working to fulfill God's promises to this broken world through us, his people.

# Notes

*Introduction: Defleshing the Human Experience*
[1]Upton Sinclair, *The Jungle* (New York: Penguin, 2006), p. 36.

*Chapter 1: Rootless, Disengaged and Screen Addicted*
[1]Richard Sennett, cited in Bryan Turner, "The Possibility of Primitiveness: Towards a Sociology of Body Marks in Cool Societies," *Body & Society* 5, nos. 2-3 (1999): 43.

[2]Zygmunt Bauman, *Liquid Love: On the Frailty of Human Bonds* (Cambridge: Polity, 2003).

[3]Ibid., pp. 207-8.

[4]All *Up in the Air* quotations are from IMDB, www.imdb.com/title/tt1193138/quotes.

[5]Charles Taylor, *Philosophy Papers, vol. 2,* Philosophy and the Human Sciences (Cambridge: Cambridge University Press, 1985), pp. 4-5.

[6]Shane L Windmeyer, "Dan and Me: My Coming Out as a Friend of Dan Cathy and Chick-fil-A," *The Huffington Post,* January 28, 2013, www.huffingtonpost.com/shane-l-windmeyer/dan-cathy-chick-fil-a_b_2564379.html.

[7]Ibid.

[8]This and the following statistics are found at "Social Media, Social Life: How Teens View Their Digital Lives," *Commonsense Media,* June 26, 2012, www.commonsensemedia.org/research/social-media-social-life/key-finding-4%3A-teens-wish-they-could-disconnect-more-often.

[9]Philip Zimbardo and Nikita Duncan, "The Demise of Guys," cited in Jim Daly, "The New TED Warns of the Demise of Guys," May 23, 2012, http://blog.ted.com/2012/05/23/new-ted-ebook-warns-of-the-demise-of-guys.

[10]John Thomson, *Living Holiness* (London: SCM Press, 2010), p. 142.

[11]Stanley Hauerwas, *The Hauerwas Reader,* ed. John Berkman and Michael Cartwright (Durham, NC: Duke University Press, 2003), p. 373.

## Chapter 2: The Schizophrenic Sense of Self

[1]Naomi Shihab Nye, "Gate A-4," in *Honeybee* (New York: Greenwillow Books, 2008), www.poets.org/viewmedia.php/prmMID/23313#sthash .VozfNmyU.dpuf.

[2]Charles Taylor, *A Secular Age* (Cambridge, MA: Harvard University Press, 2007), p. 771.

[3]Nick Page, *And Now Let's Move into a Time of Nonsense: Why Worship Songs Are Failing the Church* (London: Authentic Media, 2005), p. 41.

[4]Roger Helland and Leonard Hjalmarson, *Missional Spirituality* (Downers Grove, IL: InterVarsity Press, 2011), pp. 39-40.

[5]Doug Pagitt, *Reimagining Spiritual Formation* (Grand Rapids: Zondervan, 2003), p. 23.

[6]Michael Frost and Alan Hirsch, *The Shaping of Things to Come* (Peabody, MA: Hendrickson, 2003), pp. 18-21.

[7]Christian Smith and Melinda Lundquist Denton, *Soul Searching: The Religious and Spiritual Lives of American Teenagers* (Oxford: Oxford University Press, 2009). The same phrase is picked up in Kenda Creasy Dean's book *Almost Christian: What the Faith of Our Teenagers Is Telling the American Church* (Oxford: Oxford University Press, 2010).

[8]Smith and Denton, *Soul Searching*, p. 164.

[9]Ibid., p. 165.

[10]N. T. Wright, *Surprised by Hope* (London: SPCK, 2007), pp. 16-17.

[11]Nancey Murphy, *Bodies and Souls, or Spirited Bodies?* (Cambridge: Cambridge University Press, 2006).

## Chapter 3: Wandering Aimlessly in a Moral Minefield

[1]Dan Birlew, "Why Are Zombies So Popular?" Dan Birlew (blog), August 18, 2012, www.danbirlew.com/why-are-zombies-so-popular.

[2]"Awesome Ways to Kill Zombies!!!" *Cracked,* July 5, 2012, www.cracked .com/funny-3275-awesome-ways-to-kill-zombies212121/#ixzz1zobz6RXJ.

[3]Oliver O'Donovan, *Begotten or Made* (Oxford: Clarendon Press, 1982), p. 2.

[4]Susan Bordo, *Unbearable Weight: Feminism, Western Culture, and the Body* (Berkeley: University of California Press, 1993), p. 144.

[5]Penelope Washbourn, "Becoming Woman: Menstruation as Spiritual Challenge," in *Woman Spirit Rising: A Feminist Reader in Religion,* ed. Carol P. Christ and Judith Plaskow (New York: HarperCollins, 1992), p. 254.

[6]Kenneth Bailey, *Jesus Through Middle Eastern Eyes* (Downers Grove,

IL: InterVarsity Press, 2008), p. 136.

## Chapter 4: The Moral Ambiguity of Our Time

[1]Martin Luther King Jr., "I've Been to the Mountaintop" (speech, Bishop Charles Mason Temple, Memphis, TN, April 3, 1968), http://mlk-kpp01 .stanford.edu/index.php/encyclopedia/documentsentry/ive_been_to_the_ mountaintop/.

[2]Kyla Boyse, "Television and Children," University of Michigan Heath System, August 2010, www.med.umich.edu/yourchild/topics/tv.htm.

[3]Dave Grossman, "Trained to Kill," Killology Research Group, 2000, www .killology.com/print/print_trainedtokill.htm.

[4]"ISU Study Proves Conclusively that Violent Video Game Play Makes More Aggressive Kids," Iowa State University, March 1, 2010, http:// archive.news.iastate.edu/news/2010/mar/vvgeffects.

[5]Dave Grossman, "Trained to Kill."

[6]Albert Schweitzer, *Culture and Ethics* (Munich: Beck, 1990), p. 334.

[7]Martin Buber, *I and Thou*, trans. Ronald Gregor Smith (New York: Charles Scribner's, 1958), p. 26.

[8]Malcolm Muggeridge, cited in Dale Fincher, "Leprosy and Lust," 2005, www.soulation.org/library/articles/leprosy_and_lust.pdf.

[9]Graham Greene, cited in Zadie Smith, "Shades of Greene" *Guardian,* September 17, 2004, www.guardian.co.uk/books/2004/sep/18/classics. grahamgreene.

[10]Jens Zimmerman, *Incarnational Humanism* (Downers Grove, IL: Inter-Varsity Press, 2012), p. 35.

## Chapter 5: Religion as an Embodied Experience

[1]David Foster Wallace, "Federer as a Religious Experience," *New York Times,* August 20, 2006, www.nytimes.com/2006/08/20/sports/playmagazine/ 20federer.html?pagewanted=all.

[2]Don DeLillo, *Underworld* (New York: Scribner, 1997), pp. 15-16.

[3]John Wesley, Sunday, January 25, 1736, in *The Journal of John Wesley*, ed. Percy Livingstone Parker (Chicago: Moody Press, 1974), p. 35.

[4]Ibid., p. 36.

[5]Wesley, Tuesday, January 24, 1738, *Journal of John Wesley*, p. 53.

[6]Clarissa Pinkola Estes, *Women Who Run with the Wolves* (London: Random House, 1993), p. 200.

[7]John Wesley, preface to *The Sunday Service of the Methodists in North America,* cited in *Oxford Guide to the Book of Common Prayer,* ed. Charles Hefling and Cynthia Shattuck (Oxford: Oxford University Press, 2006), p. 210.

[8]Peter Kelley, "God Is a Drug: the Rise of American Megachurches," University of Washington, August 20, 2012, www.washington.edu/news/2012/08/20/god-as-a-drug-the-rise-of-american-megachurches.

[9]Ibid.

[10]Charles Taylor, *A Secular Age* (Cambridge, MA.: Harvard University Press, 2007), p. 613.

[11]C. S. Lewis, *Miracles* (New York: Macmillan, 1947), p. 112.

[12]Ibid., p. 117.

## Chapter 6: Learning Embodiment from the Master

[1]Graham Stanton, *The Gospels and Jesus* (Oxford: Oxford University Press, 2003), p. 201.

[2]I take these three points from Ross Langmead, *The Word Made Flesh* (Lanham, MD: University Press of America, 2004), p. 219.

[3]Karl Barth, *Dogmatics in Outline* (New York: Harper & Row, 1959), p. 21.

[4]Michael Polanyi, *Personal Knowledge* (Chicago: University of Chicago Press, 1962), p. 54.

[5]Ibid., p. 53.

[6]Lance Ford, *Unleader* (Kansas City: Beacon Hill, 2012), pp. 169-70.

[7]Kenneth Bailey, *Jesus Through Middle Eastern Eyes* (Downers Grove, IL: InterVarsity Press, 2008), p. 146.

## Chapter 7: Desire, Idolatry and Discipleship

[1]C. S. Lewis, "From the Preface to *Pilgrim's Regress,*" Whitworth University, www.whitworth.edu/Academic/Department/Philosophy/Courses/PHEL261_Baird/html/handout4.htm.

[2]C. S. Lewis, "The Weight of Glory," in *The Quotable Lewis,* ed. Wayne Martindale and Jerry Root (Wheaton, IL: Tyndale House, 1989), p. 65.

[3]Ibid.; italics added.

[4]C. S. Lewis, cited in Alister McGrath, *A Cloud of Witnesses* (Downers Grove, IL: InterVarsity Press, 2005), p. 127.

[5]Lewis, "The Weight of Glory," in *The Weight of Glory* (Grand Rapids: Eerdmans, 1949), p. 6.

[6]C. S. Lewis, *Mere Christianity* (New York: Macmillan, 1952), p. 120.

[7]James K. A. Smith, *Desiring the Kingdom* (Grand Rapids: Baker, 2009), pp. 33-34.

[8]Ibid.

[9]Charles Taylor, *Philosophy Papers, vol. 2, Philosophy and the Human Sciences* (Cambridge: Cambridge University Press, 1985), p. 113.

[10]Smith, *Desiring the Kingdom*, p. 51.

[11]Ibid., p. 54.

[12]Ibid., p. 216; italics added.

[13]Michael Frost and Alan Hirsch, *The Shaping of Things to Come* (Peabody, MA: Hendrickson, 2003), pp. 120-21.

### Chapter 8: We Are Spirited Bodies

[1]Pierre Teilhard de Chardin, *Hymn of the Universe* (London: Collins, 1961), pp. 76-77.

[2]Tim Keller, *The Reason for God* (London: Hodder & Stoughton, 2009), p. 162.

[3]Simone Weil, cited in Darcey Steinke, *Easter Everywhere: A Memoir* (London: Bloomsbury, 2007), p. 114.

[4]Keller, *Reason for God*, pp. 275-76.

[5]See Alain de Botton, *Religion for Atheists* (New York: Random House, 2012).

[6]Alan Hirsch, *The Forgotten Ways* (Grand Rapids: Brazos, 2006). See especially pp. 83-91.

[7]Nancey Murphy, *Bodies and Souls, or Spirited Bodies?* (Cambridge: Cambridge University Press, 2006), p. 3.

[8]Ibid., p. 4.

[9]Ibid., p. ix; italics added.

[10]Rowan Williams, *On Christian Theology* (Malden, MA: Blackwell, 2000), p. 239.

[11]Philip F. Sheldrake, "Christian Spirituality as a Way of Living Publicly: A Dialectic of the Mystical and Prophetic," *Spiritus* 3, no. 1 (2003): 23.

[12]Ibid., p. 24.

[13]Ibid., p. 27.

[14]Ibid., p. 33.

### Chapter 9: Mission in the Excarnate Age

[1]Micah White, "Abandon Point and Click Activism," *Adbusters*, March 18,

2009, www.adbusters.org/blogs/blackspot_blog/abandon_point_and_ click_activism.html; italics added.

[2]Mike Pflanz (April 5, 2012). "Kony2012: Part II More Solid, Moving and Accurate Presentation Than First Film," *Daily Telegraph*, April 5, 2012.

[3]Adam Gabbatt, "Kony 2012 Sequel Video—Does It Answer the Questions?" *Guardian*, April 5, 2012, www.guardian.co.uk/news/blog/2012/ apr/05/kony-2012-sequel-video-live.

[4]White, "Abandon Point and Click Activism."

[5]Robert Lupton, *Toxic Charity* (New York: HarperOne, 2011), p. 15.

[6]Ngo Menghourng, cited in David Eimer, "Voluntourism Tips: Is It Ethical to Visit Orphanages?" *Lonely Planet*, April 25, 2013, www.lonelyplanet .com/myanmar-burma/travel-tips-and-articles/77716.

[7]Ibid.

[8]Lupton, *Toxic Charity*, p. 128.

## Chapter 10: Defying Church-World Dualism

[1]David Bosch, cited in Michael Frost, *The Road to Missional* (Grand Rapids: Baker, 2011), p. 24.

[2]Micah White, "Abandon Point and Click Activism," *Adbusters*, March 18, 2009, www.adbusters.org/blogs/blackspot_blog/abandon_point_and_ click_activism.html.

[3]Robert Banks, *Redeeming the Routines: Bringing Theology to Life* (Wheaton, IL: Bridgepoint Books, 1997), pp. 50-65.

[4]William Diehl, *Christianity and Real Life* (London: Fortress, 1976), pp. v-vi, quoted in ibid., p. 59.

[5]Charles Ringma, *Catch the Wind: The Shape of the Church to Come* (Sydney: Albatross, 1994), pp. 61-62.

[6]Lesslie Newbigin, *Foolishness to the Greeks* (London: Eerdmans, 1986), p. 140.

[7]Lesslie Newbigin, *The Other Side of 1984* (Geneva: World Council of Churches, 1983), p. 40.

[8]Lesslie Newbigin, *The Gospel in a Pluralistic Society* (Grand Rapids: Eerdmans, 1989), p. 232.

[9]Bob Roberts Jr., *The Multiplying Church* (Grand Rapids: Zondervan, 2008), p. 120.

[10]I am indebted to a lecture by Reggie McNeal for these figures.

[11]David Bosch, cited in Stan Nussbaum, *A Reader's Guide to Transforming*

*Mission* (Maryknoll, NY: Orbis, 2005), p. 105.

[12]Mark Scandrette, *Practicing the Way of Jesus* (Downers Grove, IL: InterVarsity Press, 2011), pp. 77-82.

[13]Ibid., p. 77.

[14]Ibid., p. 78.

[15]Ibid., p. 81.

[16]Ibid., p. 82.

[17]Ben Saunders, "Why Bother Leaving the House?" TED, posted on YouTube, December 14, 2012, www.youtube.com/watch?feature=player_embedded&v=4jBB5iibKy0#!.

### Chapter 11: Placed Persons

[1]Jane Jacobs, *The Death and Life of Great American Cities* (New York: Penguin, 1994), p. 14; italics added.

[2]Jürgen Moltmann, *God in Creation* (Minneapolis: Fortress Press, 1993), p. 47.

[3]T. J. Gorringe, *A Theology of the Built Environment: Justice, Power, Redemption* (Cambridge: Cambridge University Press, 2002), pp. 185-92.

[4]Ibid., pp. 185-86.

[5]Maf Smith, John Whiteleg and Nick J. Williams, *Greening the Built Environment* (London: Earthscan, 1998), p. 173.

[6]Gorringe, *Theology of the Built Environment,* p. 188.

[7]Ibid.

[8]Rowan Williams, Sermon for the Southwark Diocese Centenary, July 2005, in *Faithful Cities* (London: Methodist Publishing, 2006), p. 53.

[9]Kevin Lynch, cited in Gorringe, *Theology of the Built Environment,* p. 190.

[10]Ibid.

[11]"Our Purpose," Sydney Alliance, www.sydneyalliance.org.au.

[12]Gorringe, *Theology of the Built Environment,* p. 190.

[13]Ibid., p. 92.

[14]Church of England Commission on Urban Life and Faith, *Faithful Cities* (London: Methodist Publishing, 2006), p. 16.

### Chapter 12: Adopting an Incarnational Posture

[1]Nicholas Carr, *The Shallows* (New York: Norton, 2010), p. 219.

[2]"Global Algorithm 1.7: The Silence of the Lambs, Paul Virilio in Conversation," interviewed by Paul Virilio, *Ctheory,* June 12, 1996, www.ctheory.net/articles.aspx?id=38.

[3]James Hunter, *To Change the World* (Oxford: Oxford University Press, 2010), p. 210.

[4]Ibid.

[5]Ibid.

[6]Ibid.

[7]Ibid.

[8]Ibid.

[9]Nona Willis Aronowitz, "Most Americans Want a Walkable Neighborhood, Not a Big House," *Good*, February 7, 2012, www.good.is/post/most-americans-want-a-walkable-neighborhood-not-a-big-house.

[10]Sean Benesh, *Metrospiritual* (Eugene, OR: Wipf & Stock, 2011), p. 56.

[11]Kathleen Norris, *The Cloister Walk* (London: Penguin Books, 1996), p. 244.

[12]Charles Taylor, *A Secular Age* (Cambridge, MA: Harvard University Press, 2007), p. 26.

[13]Wendell Berry, "The Futility of Global Thinking," *Harpers*, September 16, 1989, p. 22.

[14]Alan Roxburgh, "Practices of Christian Life—Forming and Performing a Culture," *Journal of Missional Practice* 1 (2012), http://themissionalnetwork .com/index.php/practices-of-christian-life-forming-and-performing-a-culture.

[15]Ibid.

[16]Ibid.

[17]Ibid.

[18]Michael Frost and Alan Hirsch, *The Shaping of Things to Come* (Peabody, MA: Hendrickson, 2003), p. 65.

[19]Wendell Berry, "Wendell Berry: The Work of the Local Culture," *The Contrary Farmer*, June 10, 2011, http://thecontraryfarmer.wordpress .com/2011/06/10/wendell-berry-the-work-of-local-culture.

### Chapter 13: The First Page of the End of Despair

[1]David Frum, quoted in Victor Bockris, "Visions of the Seventies: The Rise and Fall of a Cultural Challenge," *Gadfly*, January-February 2001, www .gadflyonline.com/archive/janfeb01/archive-seventies.html.

[2]Ibid.

[3]Ann Morisy, *Bothered and Bewildered: Enacting Hope in Troubled Times* (London: Continuum, 2009).

[4]Ibid., p. 4.

[5]Ibid., p. 8.

[6]"Healthy Religion: Psychologist, Educator, Clergyman Shares Keys to Personality and Religious Beliefs," eReleases, August 30, 2006, www.ereleases .com/pr/healthy-religion-psychologist-educator-clergyman-shares-keys-to-personality-and-religious-beliefs-8122.

[7]Don Koenig, "Christians Need to Take a Biblical Stand, for Christ's Sake!" *The Prophetic Years,* September 27, 2011, www.thepropheticyears.com/wordpress/christians-need-to-take-a-biblical-stand-for-christs-sake.html.

[8]Ibid.

[9]Morisy, *Bothered and Bewildered,* pp. 48-49.

[10]Church of England Commission on Urban Life and Faith, *Faithful Cities* (London: Methodist Publishing, 2006), p. 84.

[11]Adrienne Rich, "Dreams Before Waking," in *Your Native Land, Your Life* (New York: Norton, 1986).

## Chapter 14: Getting There

[1]Donald Miller, *Through Painted Deserts* (Nashville: Thomas Nelson, 2005), p. x.

[2]Donald Schön, *The Reflective Practitioner: How Professionals Think in Action* (New York: Basic Books, 1983).

[3]Ibid., pp. viii-ix.

[4]Ibid., p. 280.

[5]Miller, *Through Painted Deserts,* p. x.

[6]Neil Sims, "I Don't Really Have Time to Read This! Growing Through Theologically Reflective Practice," *Uniting Theology and Church* 2 (2010): 4.

[7]Ann Morisy, *Bothered and Bewildered: Enacting Hope in Troubled Times* (London: Continuum, 2009), pp. 50-51.

[8]Peter Steinke, *Congregational Leadership in Anxious Times* (Herndon, VA: Alban Institute, 2006), p. 113.

[9]Ibid., pp. 44-45.

[10]Lesslie Newbigin, *The Open Secret* (Grand Rapids: Eerdmans, 1995), pp. 33-34.

[11]René Girard, *The Scapegoat* (Baltimore: Johns Hopkins University Press, 1986).

[12]I'm indebted to Morisy, *Bothered and Bewildered,* p. 59, for this summary.

[13]Darrell J. Guder, *Unlikely Ambassadors: Clay Jar Christians in God's Service* (Louisville: Office of the General Assembly Presbyterian Church USA, 2002), p. 5.

[14]Michael Goheen, "The Urgency of Reading the Bible as One Story," *Theology Today* 64 (2008): 469-83.

[15]James Brownson, "An Adequate Missional Hermeneutic," unpublished presentation notes, cited in George Hunsberger, "Proposals for a Missional Hermeneutic: Mapping a Conversation," *Missiology* 39, no. 3 (2011): 314.

[16]Guder, *Unlikely Ambassadors*, p. 5.

[17]Ibid.

[18]Ibid.

[19]Michael Barram, "'Located Questions' for a Missional Hermeneutic," Gospel and Our Culture Network, November 1, 2006, www.gocn.org/resources/articles/located-questions-missional-hermeneutic.

[20]Hunsberger, "Proposals for a Missional Hermeneutic," p. 316.

*Epilogue: Christ in Us and We in Christ*

[1]Johnny Cash, "Wildwood in the Pines," *Personal File,* disc 2, Legacy/Columbia, 2006, recorded 1973-1982.

[2]Michael Card, "Jesus Loves Me (This I Know)," *First Light,* Milk & Honey, 1981.

[3]Pete Ward, *Liquid Church* (Peabody, MA: Hendrickson, 2002), p. 37.

[4]Charles Taylor, cited in Leon de Lomo and Bart van Leeuwen, "Charles Taylor on Secularism: Introduction and Interview," *Ethical Perspectives* 10 (2003): 84.

[5]Charles Taylor, *A Secular Age* (Cambridge, MA: Harvard University Press, 2007), p. 553.

[6]Clarissa Pinkola Estes, *Women Who Run with the Wolves* (London: Random House, 1993), p. 198.

[7]James K. A. Smith, *Desiring the Kingdom* (Grand Rapids: Baker, 2009), p. 33.

[8]Ibid.

[9]Lee Camp, *Mere Discipleship* (Grand Rapids: Brazos, 2008), p. 175.

[10]Tom Sine, cited in Heather Wraight, ed., *They Call Themselves Christians* (London: Christian Research/LCWE, 1998), p. 109.

[11]Michael Frost and Alan Hirsch, *The Faith of Leap* (Grand Rapids: Baker, 2011).

[12]Michael Frost, *Exiles* (Grand Rapids: Baker Books, 2006), pp. 150-51.

[13]Camp, *Mere Discipleship,* pp. 175-76.

[14]These values and a longer explanation of their practices can be found at

the homepage of CRM Empowering Leaders, www.crmleaders.org/teams/communitas.

[15]Christine Sine, *Return to Our Senses* (Seattle: Mustard Seed Associates, 2012).

[16]Parker J. Palmer, *Let Your Life Speak* (San Francisco: Jossey-Bass, 2000), p. 18.

[17]Kurt Vonnegut, quoted in "15 Things Kurt Vonnegut Said Better Than Anyone Else Ever Has or Will," A.V. Club, www.avclub.com/articles/15-things-kurt-vonnegut-said-better-than-anyone-el,1858.

[18]This summary is taken from Walter Brueggemann, *Cadences of Home* (Louisville: Westminster/John Knox Press, 1997).

[19]Ann Morisy, *Bothered and Bewildered: Enacting Hope in Troubled Times* (London: Continuum, 2009), p. 101.

[20]Quoted in ibid.

[21]As quoted in Brennan Manning, *The Ragamuffin Gospel* (Sisters, OR: Multnomah Books, 2005), p. 120.

**Forge**

The Forge Missions Training Network exists to help birth and nurture the missional church in America and beyond. Books published by InterVarsity Press that bear the Forge imprint will also serve that purpose.

*Creating a Missional Culture,* by JR Woodward

**Forge Guides for Missional Conversation** (set of five), by Scott Nelson

*Incarnate,* by Michael Frost

*The Missional Quest,* by Lance Ford and Brad Brisco

*More Than Enchanting,* by Jo Saxton

*Sentness,* by Kim Hammond and Darren Cronshaw

*The Story of God, the Story of Us* (book and DVD), by Sean Gladding

---

For more information on Forge America, to apply for a Forge residency, or to find or start a Forge hub in your area, visit **www.forgeamerica.com**

For more information about Forge books from InterVarsity Press, including forthcoming releases, visit **www.ivpress.com/forge**